The Man Who Had All the Luck

Arthur Miller was born in New York City in 1915. After graduating from the University of Michigan, he began work with the Federal Theatre Project. His many award-winning stage plays include *The Man Who Had All the Luck* (1944); *All My Sons* (1947); *Death of a Salesman* (1949); *An Enemy of the People* (1950), adapted from Ibsen; *The Crucible* (1953); *A Memory of Two Mondays* (1955) and *A View from the Bridge* (presented as a double bill in 1955); *After the Fall* (1964); *Incident at Vichy* (1964); *The Price* (1968); *The Creation of the World, and Other Business* (1972); *The Archbishop's Ceiling* (1977); *The American Clock* (1980); the double bills *Two-Way Mirror* (1982) and *Danger: Memory!* (1987); *The Golden Years* (written in 1940 and first performed on radio in 1987 and on television in 1991); *The Ride Down Mount Morgan* (1991); *The Last Yankee* (1993); *Broken Glass* (1994); *Mr Peters' Connections* (2000); *Resurrection Blues* (2002) and *Finishing the Picture* (2004). His other writing includes the novel *Focus* (1945) and a novella, *Plain Girl* (1995); *The Misfits* (first published in 1957 as a short story, then as a screenplay and published as a novel in 1961); *Everybody Wins* (a screenplay, published in 1990); a collection of short stories, *I Don't Need You Any More* (1967); and works of non-fiction: *In Russia* (1969); *In the Country* (1977); *Chinese Encounters* (1979); *'Salesman' in Beijing* (1984), an account of directing his best-known play in China; *'The Crucible' in History and Other Essays* (2000); *Echoes Down the Corridor: Collected Essays 1944–2000* (2000) and *On Politics and the Art of Acting* (2001). His autobiography, *Timebends, A Life*, was published in 1987. He died in February 2005 aged 89.

D1396427

Arthur Miller

The Man Who Had All the Luck

Methuen Drama

Published by Methuen Drama 2008

1 3 5 7 9 10 8 6 4 2

Methuen Drama
A & C Black Publishers Limited
38 Soho Square
London W1D 3HB
www.acblack.com

The Man Who Had All the Luck first published in Great Britain
in 1989 by Methuen London with *The Golden Years*

ISBN 978 1 408 10676 1

A CIP catalogue record for this book is available from the British Library

Typeset by Country Setting, Kingsdown, Kent
Printed and bound in Great Britain by CPI Cox & Wyman, Reading, Berkshire

The Man Who Had All The Luck was first staged at the Forrest Theater, New York, on 23 November 1944 by Joseph Fields.

The British premiere was at the Bristol Old Vic on 17 May 1990. The cast, in order of speaking, was as follows:

JB Feller	Barry Stanton
David Beeves	Iain Glen
Shory	Paul Bentall
Aunt Belle	Susan Dowdall
Patterson Beeves	Colin Farrell
Amos Beeves	David Crean
Hester Falk	Rudi Davies
Dan Dibble	Tom Durham
Andrew Falk	Christopher Robbie
Gustav Eberson	Christopher Ettridge
Augie Belfast	Christopher Robbie

Directed by Paul Unwin
Designed by Sally Crabb
Lighting by Rory Dempster
Music by Andy Sheppard

A production of *The Man Who Had All the Luck* opened at the Donmar Warehouse, London, on 28 February 2008 with the following cast:

JB Feller	Mark Lewis Jones
David Beeves	Andrew Buchan
Shory	Aidan Kelly
Aunt Belle	Sandra Voe
Patterson Beeves	Nigel Cooke
Amos Beeves	Felix Scott
Hester Falk	Michelle Terry
Dan Dibble	James Hayes
Andrew Falk	Roy Sampson
Gustav Eberson	Shaun Dingwall
Augie Belfast	Gary Lilburn

Directed by Sean Holmes
Designed by Paul Wills
Lighting by Paule Constable
Sound by Christopher Shutt

The Man Who Had All the Luck

A Fable

Characters

David Beeves
Shory
JB Feller
Andrew Falk
Patterson Beeves
Amos Beeves
Hester Falk
Dan Dibble
Gustav Eberson
Augie Belfast
Aunt Belle

The Time
Not so long ago.

Act One
Scene One *An evening in early April. Inside a barn used as a repair shop.*
Scene Two *The barn, near dawn.*

Act Two
Scene One *June. About three years later. The living room of the Falks' – now David's – house.*
Scene Two *Later that day. The living room.*

Act Three
Scene One *The following February. The living room.*
Scene Two *One month later. The living room at evening.*

Act One

Scene One

A barn in a small, midwestern town. It is set on a rake angle. The back wall of the barn sweeps towards upstage and right, and the big entrance doors are in this wall. Along the left wall a workbench on which auto tools lie along with some old parts and rags and general mechanic's junk. A rack over the bench holds wrenches, screwdrivers, other tools. In the left wall is a normal-sized door leading into Shory's Feed and Grain Store to which this barn is attached. A step-high ramp leads down from the threshold of this door into the barn. Further to the left, extending into the offstage area along the wall, are piles of cement bags. In front of them several new barrels which contain fertiliser.

Downstage, near the centre, is a small wood stove, now glowing red. Over the bench is a hanging bulb. There is a big garage jack on the floor, several old nail barrels for chairs – two of them by the stove. A large drum of alcohol lies on blocks, downstage right. Near it are scattered a few gallon tins. This is an old barn being used partly as a storage place, and mainly as an auto repair shop. The timber supports have a warm, oak colour, unstained. The colours of wood dominate the scene, and the grey of the cement bags.

Before the rise, two car horns, one of them the old-fashioned ga-goo-ga type of the old Ford, are heard honking impatiently. An instant of this and the curtain rises.

David Beeves *is filling a can from an alcohol drum. He is twenty-two. He has the earnest manner of the young, small-town businessman until he forgets it, which is most of the time. Then he becomes what he is – wondrous, funny, naive, and always searching. He wears a wind-breaker.*

Enter **JB Feller** *from the right. He is a fat man near fifty, dressed for winter. A certain delicacy of feeling clings to his big face. He has a light way of walking despite his weight.*

JB   Sure doing nice business on that alcohol, huh, David? (*Thumbing right.*) They're freezing out there, better step on it.

David   Near every car in town's been here today for some.
April! What a laugh!

JB (*nods downstage*)   My store got so cold I had to close off the
infants' wear counter. I think I'll get a revolving door for next
winter. (*Sits.*) What you got your hair all slicked for?

David (*on one knee, examines the spigot, which pours slowly*)   Going
over to Hester's in a while.

JB   Dave! (*Excitedly.*) Going alone?

David   Hester'll be here right away. I'm going to walk back
to the house with her, and . . . well, well, I guess we'll lay down
the law to him. If he's going to be my father-in-law I better
start talking to him some time.

JB (*anxiously*)   The only thing is you want to watch your step
with him.

David (*turns off spigot, lifts up can as he gets to his feet*)   I can't
believe that he'd actually start a battle with me. You think he
would?

JB   Old man Falk is a very peculiar man, Dave.

Horns sound from the right.

David (*going right with the can*)   Coming, coming!

He goes out as, from the back door, **Shory** *descends the ramp in a fury.
He is in a wheelchair. He is thirty-eight but his age is hard to tell because
of the absence of any hair on his body. He is totally bald, his beard does
not grow, his eyebrows are gone. His face is capable of great laughter and
terrible sneers. A dark green blanket covers his legs. He stops at the big
doors with his fist in the air. As he speaks the horns stop.*

Shory   Goddam you, shut those goddam horns! Can't you
wait a goddam minute?

JB   Lay off, will you? They're his customers.

Shory (*turns*)   What're you doing, living here?

JB   Why, got any objections? (*Goes to stove, clapping his arms.*)
Jesus, how can he work in this place? You could hang meat in
here. (*Warms his hands on the stove.*)

Shory   You cold with all that fat on you?

JB   I don't know why everybody thinks a fat man is always warm. There's nerves in the fat too, y'know.

Shory   Come into the store. It's warmer. Shoot some pinochle. (*Starts towards the ramp to his store.*)

JB   Dave's going over to see Falk.

Shory *stops.*

Shory   Dave's not going to Falk.

JB   He just told me.

Shory (*turns again*)   Listen. Since the day he walked into the store and asked me for a job he's been planning on going to see Falk about Hester. That's seven years of procrastination, and it ain't going to end tonight. What is it with you lately? You hang around him like an old cow or something. What'd your wife throw you out of the house again?

JB   No, I don't drink any more, not any important drinking – really. (*He sits on a barrel.*) I keep thinking about those two kids. It's so rare. Two people staying in love since they were children . . . that oughtn't to be trifled with.

Shory   Your wife did throw you out, didn't she?

JB   No, but . . . we just got the last word: no kids.

Shory (*compassionately*)   That so, Doctor?

JB   Yeh, no kids. Too old. Big, nice store with thirty-one different departments. Beautiful house. No kids. Isn't that something? You die, and they wipe your name off the mail box and . . . and that's the ballgame.

Slight pause.

(*Changing the subject; with some relish.*) I think I might be able to put Dave next to something very nice, Shor.

Shory   You're in your dotage, you know that? You're getting a Santa Claus complex.

JB No, he just reminds me of somebody. Myself, in fact.
At his age I was in a roaring confusion. And him? He's got his
whole life laid out like a piece of linoleum. I don't know why
but sometimes I'm around him and it's like watching one of
them nice movies, where you know everything is going to turn
out good . . . (*Suddenly strikes him.*) I guess it's because he's so
young . . . and I'm gettin' so goddam old.

Shory What's this you're puttin' him next to?

JB My brother-in-law up in Burley; you know, Dan Dibble
that's got the mink ranch.

Shory Oh don't bring him around, now.

JB Listen, his car's on the bum and he's lookin' for a
mechanic. He's a sucker for a mechanic!

Shory That hayseed couldn't let go of a nickel if it was
stuck up his . . .

Roar of engines starting close by outside. Enter **David** *from the upstage
door, putting a small wrench in his pocket. As he comes in, two cars are
heard pulling away. He goes to a can of gasoline and rinses his hands.*

David Geez, you'd think people could tighten a fan belt.
What time you got, John?

Shory Why, where *you* going? You can't go into Falk's
house . . .

Enter **Aunt Belle** *from the store. She is carrying a wrapped shirt and
a bag. She is a woman who was never young; skinny, bird-like, constantly
snivelling. A kerchief grows out of her hand.*

Belle I thought you were in the store. Hester said to hurry.

David (*going to her*) Oh, thanks, Belle. (*Unwrapping a shirt.*) It's
the new one, isn't it?

Belle (*horrified*) Did you want the new one?

David (*looking at the shirt*) Oh, Belle. When are you going to
remember something! Hester told you to bring my new shirt!

Belle (*lifting them out of bag*) Well I – I brought your galoshes.

David   I don't wear galoshes any more, I wanted my new shirt! Belle, sometimes you . . .

Belle *bursts into tears.*

David   All right, all right, forget it.

Belle   I only do my best, I'm not your mother.

David (*leading her right*)   I'm sorry, Aunt Belle, go – and thanks.

Belle (*still sniffling*)   Your father's got your brother Amos out running on the road . . .

David   Yeh, well . . . thanks . . .

Belle (*a kerchief at her nose*)   He makes Amos put on his galoshes, why doesn't he give a thought to you?

David (*pats her hand*)   I'll be home later.

Shory   You know why you never remember anything, Belle? You blow your nose too much. The nose is connected with the brain and you're blowin' your brains out.

David   Ah, cut it out, will ya?

With another sob, **Belle** *rushes out.*

David   She still treats me like after Mom died. Just like I was seven years old. (**David** *picks up the clean shirt.*)

Shory (*alarmed*)   Listen, that man'll kill you. (*Grabs the shirt and sits on it.*)

David (*with an embarrassed but determined laugh, trying to grab the shirt back*)   Give me that. I decided to go see him, and I'm going to see him!

Enter **Pat** *and* **Amos** *from right.* **Pat** *is a small, nervous man about forty-five,* **Amos** *is twenty-four, given to a drawl and a tendency to lumber when he walks.*

Pat (*on entering*)   What's the matter with you?

David *looks up. All turn to him as both come centre.* **Amos** *is squeezing a rubber ball.*

Pat (*pointing between* **David** *and stove*)   Don't you know better than to stand so close to that stove? Heat is ruination to the arteries.

Amos (*eagerly*)   You goin', Dave?

Shory (*to* **Pat**)   Everything was getting clear. Will you go home?

Pat   I'm his father, if you please.

Shory   Then tell him what to do, Father.

Pat   I'll tell him. (*Turns to* **David** *as though to command.*) What exactly did you decide?

David   We're going to tell Mr Andrew Falk we're getting married.

Pat   Uh-huh. Good work.

Shory   Good work! (*Pointing at* **Pat**, *he turns to* **JB**.) Will you listen to this . . . !

JB (*he shares* **Shory**'*s attitude towards* **Pat**, *but with more compassion*) But somebody ought to go along with him.

Pat (*adamantly to* **David**)   Definitely, somebody ought to go along.

Amos (*to* **David**)   Let me go. If he starts anything, I'll . . .

David (*to all*)   Now look, for Christ's sake, will you . . .

Pat (*to* **David**)   1 forbid you to curse. Close your collar, Amos. (*Of* **Amos** *to* **JB**.) Just ran two miles. (*He buttons another button on* **Amos**, *indicating his ball.*) How do you like the new method?

Amos (*holds up ball*)   Squeezin' a rubber ball.

JB   What's that, for his fingers, heh?

David *examines his arm.*

Pat   Fingers! That's the old forearm. A pitcher can have everything, but without a forearm? – Zero!

Shory (*to* **Pat**, *of* **David**)   Are you going to settle this or is he going to get himself murdered in that house?

Pat   Who? What house? (*Recalling.*) Oh yes, Dave . . .

Shory (*to* **JB**)   Oh yes, Dave! (*To* **Pat**.) You're his father, For G . . . !

David   All right. I got enough advice. Hester's coming here right away and we're going over to the house and we'll talk it out, and if . . .

Shory   His brains are busted, how are you going to talk to him? He doesn't like you, he doesn't want you, he said he'd shoot you if you came onto his place. Now will you start from there and figure it out or you going to put it together in the hospital? (*Pause.*)

David   What am I supposed to do then? Let him send her to that Normal school? I might never see her again. I know how these things work.

Shory   You don't know how these things work. Two years I waited in there for a boy to ask for the job I put up in the window. I could've made a big stink about it. I was a veteran, people ought to explain to the kids why I looked like this. But I learned something across the sea. Never go lookin' for trouble. I waited. And you came. Wait, Davey.

Pat   I'm inclined to agree with him, David.

David   I've been waiting to marry Hester since we were babies. (*Sits on a barrel.*) God! How do you know when to wait and when to take things in your hand and make them happen?

Shory   You can't make anything happen any more than a jellyfish makes the tides, David.

David   What do you say, John?

JB   I'd hate to see you battle old man Falk, but personally, Dave, I don't believe in waiting too long. A man's got to have faith, I think, and push right out into the current, and . . .

Pat (*leans forward, pointing*)   Faith, David, is a great thing. Take me, for instance. When I came back from the sea . . .

David   What time you got, John? . . . Excuse me, Dad.

JB   Twenty to eight.

David (*to* **Shory**)   You giving me that shirt or must I push you off that chair?

Pat (*continuing*)   I am speaking, David. When I came back from the sea . . .

Shory (*pointing at* **Amos**)   Before you come back from the sea, you're going to kill him, running his ass off in the snow.

Pat   Kill him! Why, it's common knowledge that pacing is indispensable for the arches. After all, a pitcher can have everything, but if his arches are not perfect . . . ?

Shory   Zero!

Pat   Before I forget, do you know if that alcohol can be used for rubbing? (*Indicates the drum.*)

David   There's only a couple of drops left.

Amos   You sold it all today? (*Joyously to* **Pat**.) I told you he'd sell it all!

Shory   Don't go making a genius out of your brother. Salesman hooked him. He bought alcohol in April when the sun was shining hot as hell.

Amos   Yeah, but look how it froze up today!

Shory   *He* didn't know it was going to freeze.

JB   Maybe he did know. (*To* **David**.) Did you, Dave?

David (*stares into his memory*)   Well, I . . . I kinda thought . . .

Pat (*breaking in*)   Speaking of geniuses, most people didn't know that there are two kinds; physical and mental. Fake pitchers like Christy Matthewson now. Or Walter Johnson. There you have it in a nutshell. Am I right, JB?

Shory   What've you got in a nutshell?

Pat (*the beginnings of confusion, his desire to protect* **Amos** *and himself against everyone, tremble in him*)   Just what I said. People simply refuse to concentrate. They don't know what they're supposed to be doing in their lives.

Shory (*pointing to* **David**)   Example number one.

Pat (*rises to a self-induced froth of a climax*)   I always left David to concentrate for himself. But take Amos then. When I got back from the sea I came home and what do I find? An infant in his mother's arms. I felt his body and I saw it was strong. And I said to myself, this boy is not going to waste out his life being seventeen different kind of things and ending up nothing. He's going to play baseball. And by ginger he's been throwin' against the target down the cellar seven days a week for twelve solid years! That's concentration! That's faith! That's taking your life in your own hands and moulding it to fit the thing you want. That's bound to have an effect . . . and don't you think they don't know it!

Shory   Who knows it?

Pat (*with a cry*)   I don't like everybody's attitude! (*Silence an instant. All staring at him.*) It's still winter! Can he play in the winter?

Shory   Who are you talking about?

David (*going away – towards the right – bored and disgusted*)   Dad, he didn't say . . .

Pat   He doesn't have to say it. You people seem to think he's going to go through life pitching Sundays in the sand lots. (*To all.*) Pitching's his business; it's a regular business like . . . like running a store, or being a mechanic or anything else. And it happens that in the winter there is nothing to do in his business but sit home and wait!

JB   Well, yeh, Pat, that's just what he ought to be doing.

Pat   Then why does everybody look at him as though . . . ?

He raises his hand to his head, utterly confused and ashamed for his outburst. A long pause like this.

David (*unable to bear it, he goes to* **Pat**)   Sit down, Dad. Sit down. (*He gets a barrel under* **Pat**, *who sits, staring, exhausted.*)

Pat   I can't understand it. Every paper in the county calls him a phenomenon.

As he speaks, **David**, *feeling* **Pat**'s *pain, goes right a few yards and stands looking away.*

Pat   Undefeated. He's ready for the big leagues. Been ready for three years. Who can explain a thing like that? Why don't they send a scout?

David   I been thinking about that, Dad. Maybe you ought to call the Detroit Tigers again.

Amos (*peevishly. This has been in him a long time*)   He never called them in the first place.

Pat   Now, Amos.

David (*reprimanding*)   Dad . . .

Amos   He didn't. He didn't call them. (*To* **Pat**.) I want him to know!

David (*to* **Pat**)   But last summer you said . . .

Pat   I've picked up the phone a lot of times . . . but I . . . I wanted it to happen . . . naturally. It ought to happen naturally, Dave.

Shory   You mean you don't want to hear them say no.

Pat   Well . . . yes, I admit that. (*To* **David**.) If I call now and demand an answer, maybe they'll have to say no. I don't want to put that word in their head in relation to Amos. It's a great psychological thing there. Once they refuse it's twice as hard to get them to accept.

David   But, Dad, maybe. . . maybe they forgot to send a scout. Maybe they even thought they'd sent one and didn't, and when you call they'll thank you for reminding them. (*To all.*) I mean . . . can you *just wait for something to happen?*

Shory (*claps*)   Pinochle? Let's go. Come on, John! Pat!

They start for the store door.

JB (*glancing at his watch*)   My wife'll murder me.

Shory   Why? Pinochle leaves no odour on the breath.

Pat (*turning at ramp*)   I want you to watch us, Amos. Pinochle is very good for the figuring sense. Help you on base play. Open your coat.

Pat *follows* **Shory** *and* **JB** *into store.* **Amos** *dutifully starts to follow, hesitates at the door, then closes it behind them and comes to* **David**.

Amos   Dave, I want to ask you something. (*He glances towards the door, then quietly.*) Take me over, will ya? (**David** *just looks at him.*) Do something for me. I'm standing still. I'm not going anywhere. I swear I'm gettin' ashamed.

David   Ah, don't, don't, Ame.

Amos   No, I am. Since I started to play everybody's been saying, (*Mimics.*) 'Amos is goin' some place, Amos is goin' someplace.' I been out of high school five years and I'm still taking spending money. I want to find a girl. I want to get married. I want to start doing things. You're movin' like a daisy cutter, Dave, you know how to *do*. Take me over.

David   But I don't know half what Pop knows about baseball . . . about training or . . .

Amos   I don't care, you didn't know anything about cars either, and look what you made here.

David   What'd I make? I got nothin'. I still don't know anything about cars.

Amos   But you do. Everybody knows you know . . .

David   Everybody's crazy. Don't envy me, Ame. If every car I ever fixed came rolling in here tomorrow morning and the guys said I did it wrong I wouldn't be surprised. I started on

Shory's Ford and I got another one and another, and before I knew what was happening they called me a mechanic. But I ain't a trained man. You are. You *got* something . . . (*Takes his arm, with deepest feeling.*) and you're going to be great. Because you deserve it. You know something perfect. Don't look to me, I could be out on that street tomorrow morning, and then I wouldn't look so smart . . . Don't laugh at Pop. You're his whole life, Ame. You hear me? You stay with him.

Amos   Gee, Dave . . . you always make me feel so good. (*Suddenly like* **Pat**, *ecstatic.*) When I'm in the leagues I'm gonna buy you . . . a . . . a whole goddam garage!

Enter **Hester** *from the right. She is a full-grown girl, a heartily developed girl. She can run fast, swim hard and lift heavy things – not stylishly, but with the most economic and direct way to run, swim and lift. She has a loud, throaty laugh. Her femininity dwells in one fact – she loves* **David** *with all her might, always has, and she doesn't feel she's doing anything when he's not around. The pallor of tragedy is nowhere near her. She enters breathless, not from running but from expectation.*

Hester   David, he's home. (*Goes to* **David** *and cups his face in her hands.*) He just came back! You ready? (*Looks around* **David**'s *shoulder at* **Amos**.) Hullo, Ame, how's the arm?

Amos   Good as ever.

Hester   You do that long division I gave you?

Amos   Well, I been working at it.

Hester   There's nothing better'n arithmetic to sharpen you up. You'll see, when you get on the diamond again, you'll be quicker on base play. We better go, David.

Amos (*awkwardly*)   Well . . . good luck to ya. (*He goes to the store door.*)

David   Thanks, Ame.

Amos *waves, goes through the door and closes it behind him.*

Hester   What're you looking so pruney about? Don't you want to go?

David   I'm scared, Hess. I don't mind tellin' you. I'm scared.

Hester   Of a beatin'?

David   You know I was never scared of a beatin'.

Hester   We always knew we'd have to tell him, didn't we?

David   Yeh, but I always thought that by the time we had to, I'd be somebody. You know.

Hester   But you are somebody . . .

David   But just think of it from his side. He's a big farmer, a hundred and ten of the best acres in the county. Supposing he asks me – I only got three hundred and ninety-four dollars, counting today.

Hester   But we always said, when you had three fifty we'd ask him.

David   God, if I was a lawyer, or a doctor, or even a book-keeper.

Hester   A mechanic's good as a book-keeper!

David   Yeh . . . but I don't know if I am a mechanic. (*Takes her hand.*) Hess, listen, in a year maybe I could build up some kind of a real business, something he could look at and see.

Hester   A year! Davey, don't . . . don't you. . . ?

David   I mean . . . let's get married now, without asking him.

Hester   I told you, I can't . . .

David   If we went away . . . far, far away . . .

Hester   Wherever we went, I'd always be afraid he'd knock on the door. You don't know what he can do when he's mad. He roared my mother to her grave . . . We have to face him with it, Davey. It seems now that I've known it since we were babies. When I used to talk to you at night through the kitchen window, when I'd meet you to ride around the quarry in Shory's car; even as far back as *The Last of the Mohicans* in 6B. I always knew we'd have to sit in the house together and listen to him roaring at us. We have to, Davey. (*She steps away, as though to give him a choice.*)

David (*he smiles, a laugh escapes him*)   You know, Hess, I don't only love you. You're my best friend.

Hester *springs at him and kisses him. They are locked in the embrace when a figure enters from the right. It is* **Dan Dibble**, *a little sun-dried farmer, stolidly dressed – a mackinaw, felt hat. He hesitates a moment, then . . .*

Dibble   Excuse me . . . JB Feller . . . is JB Feller in here?

David   JB? Sure. (*Points at back door.*) Go through there . . . he's in the store.

Dibble   Much obliged.

David   That's all right, sir.

Dibble *ups his hat slightly to* **Hester**, *goes a few yards towards the door, turns.*

Dibble   You . . . you Dave Beeves? Mechanic?

David   Yes, sir, that's me.

Dibble *nods, turns, goes up the ramp and into the store, closing door behind him.* **David** *looks after him.*

Hester   Come, Davey.

David   Yeh. I'll get my coat. (*He goes to rail at back where it hangs, starts to put it on.*) Gosh, I better change my shirt. Shory grabbed my clean one before. I guess he took it into the store with him.

Hester (*knowingly*)   He doesn't think you ought to go.

David   Well . . . he was just kiddin' around. I'll only be a minute.

David *starts for the store door when it opens and* **JB** *surges out full of excitement.* **Dibble** *follows him, then* **Amos**, *then* **Pat**, *and finally* **Shory** *who looks on from his wheelchair above the ramp.*

JB   Hey, Dave! Dave, come here. (*To* **Dan**.) You won't regret it, Dan . . . Dave . . . want you to meet my brother-in-law from up in Burley. Dan Dibble.

David   Yes, sir, how de do.

JB   Dan's got a brand new Marmon . . . he's down here for a funeral, see, and he's staying at my house.

David (*to* **JB**. *A note of faltering*)   Marmon, did you say?

JB   Yeh, Marmon. (*Imperatively.*) You know the Marmon, Dave.

David   Sure, ya . . . (*To* **Dibble**.) Well, bring it around. I'll be glad to work on her. I've got to go right now.

JB   Dan, will you wait in my car? Just want to explain a few things, I'll be right out and we'll go.

Dibble   Hurry up. It's cold out there. I'd like him to get it fixed up by tomorrow. It's shakin' me up so, I think I'm gettin' my appendix back.

JB (*jollying him to the door*)   I don't think they grow back once they're cut out.

Dibble   Well, it feels like it. Be damned if I'll ever buy a Marmon again. (**Dibble** *goes out.*)

JB (*he comes back to* **David**)   This idiot is one of the richest farmers in the Burley district . . . He's got that mink ranch I was tellin' you about.

David   Say, I don't know anything about a Marmon . . .

JB   Neither does he. He's got two vacuum cleaners in his house and never uses nothin' but a broom. Now listen. He claims she ain't hittin' right. I been tryin' the past two weeks to get him to bring her down here to you. Now get this. Besides the mink ranch he's got a wheat farm with five tractors.

Hester   Five tractors!

JB   He's an idiot, but he's made a fortune out of mink. Now you clean up this Marmon for him and you'll open your door to the biggest tractor farms in the state. There's big money in tractor work, you know that. He's got a thousand friends and they follow him. They'll follow him here.

David   Uh-huh. But I don't know anything about tractors.

Hester   Oh, heck, you'll learn!

David   Yeah, but I can't learn on his tractors.

Hester   Yeah, but . . .

JB   Listen! This could be the biggest thing that ever happened to you. The Marmon's over at my house. He's afraid to drive her any further on the snow. I'll bring her over and you'll go to work. All right?

David   Yeah, but look, John, I . . .

JB   You better get in early and start on her first thing in the morning. All right?

Hester (*with a loud bubble of laughter*)   David, that's wonderful!

David (*quickly*)   See, if we waited, Hess. In six months, maybe less, I'd have something to show!

Hester   But I'm going to Normal in a week if we don't do it now!

Shory   You're pushing him, Hester.

Hester (*a sudden outburst at* **Shory**)   Stop talking to him! A person isn't a frog, to wait and wait for something to happen!

Shory   He'll fight your father if you drag him there tonight! And your father can kill him!

David (*takes her hand. Evenly*)   Come on, Hess. We'll go. (*To* **JB**.) Bring the car over, I'll be back later . . .

But **JB** *is staring off right, down the driveway.* **David** *turns, with* **Hester** *and all, to follow his stare. She steps a foot away from him. Enter* **Andrew Falk**, *a tall, old man, hard as iron, near-sighted, slightly stooped. Sound of idling motor outside.*

JB (*after a moment*)   I'll bring the car, Dave. Five minutes.

David (*affecting a businesslike, careless flair*)   Right, JB, I'll fix him up. (*As* **JB** *goes out.*) And thanks loads, John!

Falk *has been looking at* **Hester**, *who dares every other moment to look up from the floor at him.* **David** *turns to* **Falk**, *desperately controlling his voice.* **Pat** *enters from* **Shory**'s *store.*

David   Evening, Mr Falk. You want to go in to Shory's store? There's chairs there . . . (**Falk** *turns deliberately, heavily looks at him.*) You left your engine running. Stay awhile. Let me shut it off.

Falk   You willin' to push it?

David   Oh, battery run down?

Falk (*caustically*)   I don't know what else would prevent her from turnin' over without a push. (*To* **Hester**.) I'll see you home.

Hester (*smiling, she goes to him, but does not touch him*)   We were just comin' to the house, Daddy.

Falk   Go on home, Hester.

David   We'd like to talk to you, Mr Falk. (*Indicating the store.*) We could all go.

Falk (*in reply*)   Go on home, Hester.

David (*with a swipe at indignation*)   I'd like for her to be here, Mr Falk . . .

Falk (*he does not even look at* **David**)   I'll be home right away. (*He takes her arm and moves her to the right. She digs her heels in.*)

Hester (*a cry*)   Daddy, why . . . !

She breaks off, looking into his face. With a sob she breaks from him and runs off right. He turns slowly to **David**, *takes a breath.*

David (*angering*)   That ain't gonna work any more, Mr Falk. We're old enough now.

Pat (*reasonably*)   Look, Falk, why don't we . . . ?

Falk (*to* **David**, *without so much as a glance at* **Pat**)   This is the last time I'm ever goin' to talk to you, Beeves. You . . .

David   Why is it you're the only man who hates me like this? Everybody else . . .

Falk   Nobody but me knows what you are.

Shory (*from the store doorway*)   What is he? What are you blowin' off about?

Falk (*his first rise of voice. He points at* **Shory**)   The good God gave you your answer long ago! Keep your black tongue in your head when I'm here.

Shory (*nervously. To* **David**)   His brains are swimmin', don't you see? What are you botherin' with him for . . . !

Falk (*roaring, he takes a stride towards* **Shory**)   Shut up, you . . . you whoremonger! You ruined your last woman on *this* earth! The good God saw to that.

Shory (*with a screech of fury*)   You don't scare me, Falk. You been dead twenty years, why don't you bury yourself?

Falk *strangely relaxes, walks away from* **Shory**'s *direction, raising his shoulder to run his chin on his coat collar. The motor outside stalls. His head cocks towards right.*

David (*pointing to the right*)   Your car stalled. I'll start her up for you.

Falk   Don't touch anything I own! (*Pause.*) What were you doin' that night I caught you with her by the river? You got backbone enough to tell me that?

David (*recalls*)   Oh . . . we were kids then. . . just talkin', that's all.

Falk   You never come and ask me if she could talk to you. You come sneakin' every time, like a rat through the fences.

David   Well . . . Hess was always scared to ask you, and I . . . I guess I got it from her.

Falk   You're scared of me now too, and you know why,
Beeves? Nobody but me knows what you are.

David   Why, what am I?

Falk   You're a lost soul, a lost man. You don't know the
nights I've watched you, sittin' on the river ice, fishin' through
a hole – alone, alone like an old man with a boy's face. Or
makin' you a fire in Keldon's woods where nobody could see.
And that Sunday night you nearly burned down the church . . .

David   I was nowhere near the church that night . . . !

Falk   It couldn't have been nobody else! When the church
burned there never was a sign from God that was so clear.

Amos   He was down the cellar with me when the church
burned.

Falk (*looks at* **Amos**)   I am not blind. (*Turns back to* **David**.)
The man Hester marries is gonna know what he's about. He's
gonna be a steady man that I can trust with what I brought
forth in this world. He's gonna know his God, he's gonna know
where he came from and where he's goin'. You ain't that man.
(*He turns to go.*)

David   I'm marryin' Hester, Mr Falk. (**Falk** *stops, turns.*) I'm
sorry, but we're going to marry.

Falk   Beeves, if you ever step onto my land again, I'll put a
bullet through you, may God write my words . . . I don't fool,
Beeves. Don't go near her again. (*Points to* **Shory**.) No man
who could find a friend in that lump of corruption is going to
live in my daughter's house. (*He starts to go again.*)

David   I'm marryin' Hester, Mr Falk! We're gonna do it!

Falk   You'll sleep with your shroud first, Beeves. I'm old
enough to know what I'll do. Stay away!

*He goes to the right edge of the stage and hesitates, looking off right in the
direction of his stalled car.* **David** *starts doubtfully towards him, looking
over his shoulder.*

Shory (*rolling down the ramp*) Let him start it himself! Don't be a damned fool!

Falk *hurries out.*

Pat (*pointing right*) Maybe you ought to give him a push.

Shory Not on your life! (*He pushes himself between* **David** *and the door.*) Get away from there, go on!

David (*looking off right all the time*) Shory . . . he's going . . . what can I say to him . . . (*Starts to go right.*) I'll help him.

Shory (*pushes him back*) Get away! (*Calling off right.*) That's it, Grandpa, push it . . . push it! Harder, you crazy bastard, it's only half a mile! Go ahead, harder! (*Laughs wildly, mockingly.*)

David (*wrenches the chair around*) Stop it!

Shory You can't talk to that man! You're through, you damned fool.

David (*suddenly*) Come on, Ame, we'll pick up Hester on the road before he gets home. I'm going to do it tonight, by God.

Amos (*in ecstasy at the thought of action, he wings the ball across the stage*) Let's go!

Pat (*grabs* **David**) No, Dave . . .

David (*furiously*) No, I gotta do it, Dad!

Pat I forbid it. (*To* **Amos**.) I forbid you to go. (*To* **David**.) She's his daughter and he's got a right, David.

David What right has he got! *She* wants me!

Pat Then let her break from him. That's not your province.

David She's scared to death of him! The whole thing is between me and Hester. *I don't understand why I can't have that girl!*

Shory (*sardonically*) Must there be a reason?

David (*he stops for an instant as though a light flashed on him*) Yes, there has to be a reason! I did everything a man could do. *I didn't do anything wrong and . . .*

Shory You didn't have to! (**David** *stares at* **Shory**.) A man is a jellyfish. The tide goes in and the tide goes out. About what happens to him, a man has very little to say. When are you going to get used to it?

David *stands staring.*

Pat You better go home and sleep, Dave. Sleep is a great doctor, you know.

Shory (*gently*) He said it, Dave.

Enter **JB** *in a hurry.*

JB Where is Dan? Where's the Marmon?

Pat He didn't come here.

JB That ox! I tell him I'll drive it over for him. No, Dan Dibble don't allow anybody behind the wheel but himself. I go into the house to tell Ellie I'm goin' and when I come out he's gone. (*Starts to go right.*) That seven-passenger Marmon . . .

David He probably decided to go back home to Burley.

JB No, I'm sure he's tryin' to get here. Rugged individualist! I'll find him on some dirt road some place . . . (*He shuts up abruptly as a door slams outside.*)

All look right.

David (*alarmed*) Hester!

He quickly goes off right. For an instant **Amos**, **Pat** *and* **Shory** *are galvanised.* **Amos** *goes off and returns immediately supporting* **Dan Dibble** *who is shaking all over and seems about to collapse in distress.*

Dibble (*on entering*) God help me, God in Heaven help me . . .

Enter **David** *and* **JB** *helping* **Hester**. *She is sobbing on* **David**'s *arm and he is trying to lift her face up.*

David Stop crying, what's the matter? Hester, stop it, what happened? JB!

Dibble (*goes prayerfully to* **Hester**) I couldn't see him, Miss, how in the world could I see him? His car had no lights . . .

Hester's *loud sob cuts him off.*

David (*to* **Dibble**)   What happened? What did you do?

Dibble   Oh, God in Heaven, help me . . .

JB (*goes to him, pulls his hands down*)   Dan . . . stop that. For Pete's sake, what happened?

Dibble   This girl's father . . . an old man . . . I couldn't see him . . . He was pushing a car without lights. There were no lights at all, and he walked out from behind just as I came on him.

But for **Hester***'s subsiding sobs, there is silence for a moment. She looks at* **David***, who looks once at her, then comes to life.*

David (*to* **Dibble**)   Where is he now?

Dibble (*points upstage*)   I took him to his house . . . she was there. It happened a few feet from his house.

David (*horrified*)   Well, why didn't you get a doctor! (*He starts for the back door.*)

Hester   No . . . he's dead, Davey.

Almost at the ramp, **David** *stops as though shot. After an instant he turns quickly. He comes as in a dream a few yards towards her, and, as in a dream, halts, staring at her.*

Hester   He's dead.

David *stares at her. Then turns his head to* **Pat**, **Amos**, **Shory**, **Dibble** . . . *as though to seek reality. Then looking at her once more he goes to the nail barrel and sits.*

David (*whisper*)   I'll be darned. (*Goes to* **Hester** . . . *after a moment.*) I'm so sorry.

Hester   It was nobody's fault. Oh that poor man!

Pat (*goes to* **David**)   You better . . . come home, David.

David (*he gets up, goes to* **Hester**, *takes her hand*)   Hess? I really am sorry.

Hester *looks at him, a smile comes to her face. She thankfully throws her arms around him and sobs.*

David   Don't, Hess . . . don't cry any more. Please, Hess . . . John, take her to your house for tonight, heh?

JB   I was going to do that. (*Takes* **Hester**'s *arm.*) Come on, baby. I'll tend to everything.

David   Goodnight, Hess. You sleep, heh?

Hester   You mustn't feel any fault, Davey.

David   I could have gotten him started, that's all. He said . . . (*A filament of sardonic laughter.*) 'Don't touch anything I own.'

Hester   It wasn't your fault! You understand? In any way.

David (*nods inconclusively*)   Go to bed, go ahead.

JB (*leading* **Hester** *off*)   We'll get you home, and you'll sleep.

Dibble (*follows them until he gets to the right edge. Turning to* **David**) If there's any blood on the car, will you clean it off? Please, will you?

Dibble *goes,* **David** *looks after them.*

Shory   Get me home, will you, Dave?

David   Huh? No, I'll stay awhile. I want to look at the car. You take him, will you, Dad?

Pat (*taking hold of the back of* **Shory**'s *chair*)   Sure. Come on, Amos.

Shory   Well, wake up, jellyfish. A hundred and ten of the best acres in the valley. Not bad, eh?

David (*stunned*)   Just like that.

Shory   Never happens any other way, brother. (*Almost intones it.*) Jellyfish don't swim . . . It's the tide moves him out and in . . . out and in . . . and in. Keep it in mind. (*To* **Pat**.) Let's go, Father.

They push him out as **David** *stands there lost in a dream.*

Curtain.

Scene Two

The barn near dawn.

David *is lying under the front end of the Marmon. Beside it the hood stands on end on the floor.* **David** *is lying under the engine with one light near his head, hurriedly tightening a nut on the pan. There is one other light on, over the bench, but this is shaded. After a moment,* **David** *hurriedly slides out from under and, eagerly looking at the engine, wipes his hands. He is about to get into the car to start it when a soft knock from offstage right is heard. Startled, he peers through the darkness.*

David   Who's that? (*Surprised.*) Hester.

Hester (*she comes out of the darkness at right*)   Aren't you finished yet?

David (*glancing defensively at the car*)   What are you doing up? What time is it?

Hester   It's almost five. I called your house, I just couldn't sleep. Belle said you were still here. Can I watch you?

David   . . . It's pretty cold in here, you'll catch cold.

Hester (*she goes to him, takes his face in her hands, and kisses him*) You didn't kiss me yet.

David (*with growing ill-ease*)   Please, Hess, I gotta figure something out here. I wish . . . I wish you'd leave me alone for a while. Please.

Hester (*with quiet astonishment – and compassion*)   Haven't you figured it out yet?

David   Oh, I got it just about, but not . . . (*Stops.*) Hess, please leave me alone.

He walks from her and pretends to study the engine.

Hester   Davey.

David   Ya?

Hester   You're *going* to be able to fix it, aren't you?

David   Don't you think I can?

Hester I know you can.

David Then why do you ask me?

Hester Because . . . in the Burley garage they didn't know how to fix it.

David (*he straightens. Slight pause*) How do you know?

Hester JB told me. He's going to tell you in the morning after you're finished. He didn't want to scare you about it.

David (*with growing fear*) That can't be. They got regular trained mechanics in the Burley garage.

Hester But it's true. Mr Dibble said they wanted to take the whole thing apart and charge him a hundred and fifty dollars, and he wouldn't let them because . . .

David (*comes to her anxiously*) Why'd they want to take the whole thing apart?

Hester (*seeing his bewilderment clearer*) Well, I don't know, Davey.

David Well, what'd they tell him was wrong? Don't you remember . . . ?

Hester (*her sob threatening*) Well, Davey, don't shout at me that way, I don't know anything about cars . . . (*She begins to cry.*)

David (*with the pain of guilt*) Oh, Hester, don't cry, please. I'll fix it, I'll find out what the matter is, please, stop it, will you?

The pain it causes him makes him turn and almost march to the car. On the point of weeping himself.

I never *heard* an engine make that sound. I took the pan off, I took the head off, I looked at the valves; I just don't know what it is, Hess! It's turning off-centre somewhere and I can't find it, I can't!

Hester (*her sobbing vanishes as she senses his loss*) That's all right, Davey, it'll be all right. Maybe you better go to bed. You look so tired . . . It really doesn't matter so much.

David (*she growing taller upon his guilt*)   Gosh, Hess . . . there never was a girl like you. (*He goes to her and kisses her.*) I swear there never was.

Hester   Don't ever try for anything I want, if it worries you too much to get it, Davey.

David (*he kisses her cheek. With swift resolution*)   You go home and go to bed. I'll find out what's the matter. I'll do it! You go.

Hester   All right, Davey, 'cause JB was telling Mr Dibble such great things about you . . . He's got a marvellous thing to tell you in the morning.

David   What?

Hester   I can't tell you till you finish . . .

David   Please, Hess, what'd he say?

Hester   No, fix it first. (*Pause.*) JB wants to tell you himself. He made me promise. Goodnight.

David   Goodnight, Hess.

Hester (*going and waving*)   And don't worry . . . about anything, okay?

David   . . . I won't.

He watches her go, then turns to the car, goes and stands over it, tapping his nose with his finger thoughtfully. Then lightly punching his fist into his palm in the heartbeat rhythm, faster, then faster . . . then . . . Bursting out in loud whisper.

God damn!

The sound of a man walking into the shop rather slowly from offstage right is heard. **David** *turns towards the sound and stands still, watching.* **Gustav Eberson** *enters. He is a strong man, his suit is pressed but too small for him. He wears a white shirt. A plain brown overcoat. He is smiling warmly, but with the self-effacing manner of an intruder.* **David** *says nothing as he approaches.*

Gus (*a slight German accent*)   Excuse me, are you Mr Beeves?

David   Yeh. (*Slight pause.*)

Gus   My name is Eberson . . . Gus Eberson . . . (*With an apologetic nod and smile.*) Are you very busy? I could of course come back. Four o'clock in the morning is not the best time to visit.

David   I'm busy . . . but what can I do for you?

Gus   I moved into town last night. And I couldn't wait to see my first morning. I noticed your light. I thought we ought to know each other.

David (*taken*)   I'm glad to know you. I was almost hoping you were a hold-up man and you'd knock me unconscious.

Gus   I didn't mean to walk in so invisibly; I am opening a repair garage on the other end of the avenue.

David   Repair garage? You mean to repair cars?

Gus (*earnestly, worriedly*)   I want to assure you, Mr Beeves, that if I didn't think there is plenty of business here for both of us I would never set up a place in this town.

David (*a faint tightness cramps his voice*)   Oh, there's plenty of business for two here. Plenty! Where is your shop?

Gus   Over there on Poplar Street, right next to the grocery store.

David   Oh, that place. Gosh, nobody's been in that building for years. We used to say it was haunted.

Gus   Maybe it is! (*Laughs lightly at himself.*)   I have very little machinery. As a matter of fact . . . (*Quite happily.*) I have very little money too. So possibly I will not be troubling you very long.

David (*with emphatic assurance*)   Oh, you'll make out all right. (*Vaguely indicates the shop.*) There's nothin' to it. You come from around here?

Gus   No, I was with the Ford's Company, the River Rouge plant for several years. This last year and four months I was by the Hudson Motor people.

David (*breathlessly*)   Well . . . I guess you oughta know your stuff.

Gus (*sensing . . . extra hearty, therefore*)   What is there to know? You are probably much better than I am!

David   No, that's all right, I just meant . . .

Gus   I am not in the world to become rich. I was doing very well in Detroit.

David   Then why'd you come here?

Gus   It is my nature. I cannot get used, I shall run, run, run, I shall work, work, work, all the time rushing. To tell you the truth, I was five years with Ford's and not one good friend did I have. Here, I hope, it will be more conducive to such activities as I always enjoy. A small town and so forth. I am Austrian, you understand . . . Meanwhile I hope you will not object too strongly of my arrival?

David (*entranced*)   Hell no. Lots of luck to you! I got no right to object. (*Extends his hand jerkily.*)

Gus (*shakes hands*)   Rights is not the question. I want to be welcome. Otherwise I will . . .

David (*softly;* **Gus** *holds onto his hand*)   No . . . You're welcome here . . . You are.

Gus   Thank you . . . Thank you.

Laughs softly, thankfully. Their hands part. **Gus** *turns a slow full circle looking at the shop.* **David** *watches him like a vision. At last the Austrian faces him again. Quietly.*

Gus   How old are you?

David   Goin' on twenty-two.

Gus (*indicating the car, the shop . . . everything*)   How . . . how did you know what to do? You studied somewhere mechanics?

David (*with pride and yet uneasiness. The Austrian has grown very tall in his eyes*)   Oh no − I just picked it up kinda. (*Wanders near the Marmon as though to hide it.*) But I guess I got plenty to learn.

Gus   No, no! The best mechanics is made in this fashion. You must not feel at all . . . how shall I say . . . at a loss.

Pause. They hold each other's gaze in a moment of understanding. Slowly the Austrian's eyes turn towards the Marmon. **David**, *as though relinquishing it, moves aside now, not screening it any longer.*

Gus   What's his trouble?

David (*still entranced, and yet he must laugh as he confesses*)   You got me there. I've been at it all night.

Gus (*sauntering easily to the car*)   Oh? What he complains of?

David (*for a moment he holds back; then the last shred of resentment fades and he bursts out*)   She runs with a peculiar kind of a shudder . . . like a rubbing somewhere inside.

Gus   She misfires?

David   That's what's so funny. She fires on eight and the carburettor's set right on the button.

Pause. **Gus** *looks down at the engine.* **David** *is bent over watching his face.*

Gus   If you . . . feel like it, you can start the engine.

David (*looks at him in silence*)   You . . . you know what it is?

Gus (*reaches to him quickly*)   Look, boy, tell me and I will leave the town, I'll never come back.

David   No, no . . . I want it to be . . . just the way it ought to be, the way it . . . happened.

David *goes to car door, gets in − starts the motor. The Austrian stands listening for five seconds, then snaps his hand for the motor to be switched off. It is quiet again.* **David** *comes slowly out of the car and stands beside the Austrian, watching him.*

Gus   It is very rare. In a car so new. It comes sometimes with the Marmon, however.

David (*softly*)   What is it?

Gus (*turns straight to him*)   The crankshaft is sprung.

David (*for a long moment he stares into the Austrian's face*)   How could you tell by listening?

Gus   Same way you do for pistons. You know. You going to work now?

David (*looks at the car*)   Ya.

He hurries around the front of the car, picks up a wrench, comes around and sets the wrench on a heat nut and starts forcing it.

Gus (*hesitates for a moment, then lays his hand on* **David**)   Don't take the head off. (**David** *stops.*) I mean . . . you don't need to, necessarily. (**David** *stops moving. The wrench clatters out of his hand. He stands nearly trembling before the Austrian, who suddenly turns.*) I'll go.

David (*stops him*)   No, I always knew a time would come when . . . this would happen. I mean somebody like you would come, and then I'd just . . . pack up. I knew it all the time . . .

Gus   That's nonsense. You fixed plenty cars no doubt; you're a mechanic . . .

David   No, I'm not really. I don't know anything about metals and ratios and . . . I was almost going to tow it to the shop in Newton. Would you tell me what to do?

Gus   Gladly. And maybe sometimes I need a hand you'll drop by. All right?

David   Oh, I'd be glad to.

Gus (*grips his shoulder and points under the car*)   First you take the pan down.

David (*slight pause*)   Ya?

Gus   Then you drop the bearings. Label them so you know where to put them back.

David   Ya?

Gus   Then you drop the main bearings for the crankshaft.

David   Ya?

Gus   Then you drop the shaft itself. Take it up to Newton, is a good shop there. Tell them to exchange for a new shaft.

David   Can't I straighten this one?

Gus   Is not possible for you.

David   Could you straighten it?

Gus   That would depend – but I sold my instruments for this. You go to work now. Go ahead. ·

David (*starts to move*)   You in a hurry to go away?

Gus   I'll stay, I'll watch you.

David (*thankfully*)   Okay. (*He gets down on his knees and is about to get under the car.*) You feel like workin'? Just for a couple of minutes?

Gus   You would like me to?

David   I always wanted to see how somebody else works. Y'know?

Gus   All right, come on. We rip her open. (*He pulls off his coat.*) You got a socket, a quarter-inch?

David (*a new excitement in him*)   I ain't got sockets yet, but . . .

Gus   That's all right, give me an open end. (**David** *goes for the wrench quickly.*) How much oil you got in here?

David (*finding the wrench*)   Just a couple of quarts. I just ran her a minute. I'll drain her.

He gets under car quickly, opening the drain nuts, setting a can under it, as . . .

Gus   Are you married?

David   Not yet . . . (*Under the car.*) But pretty soon . . . are you?

Gus (*ready to work, he kneels on one knee beside the car*)   No, but I am always hopeful. There is a nice red-headed girl in this town? (*Preparing to slide under.*)

David (*laughs*)   She got to be red-headed?

Gus   Yes, I would prefer such a colour. It always seemed to me in a small American town would be many red-headed girls. Probably this is because in general I like a small town. When this car has to be ready? (*Slides under.*)

David *moves to make room; sits on his heels beside the car.*

David   Eleven in the morning, if possible. You think it can?

Gus   Oh, plenty of time. You got a car to take this shaft to Newton?

David   Yeh, that Ford outside. Oh – my back.

Gus   Spread out, take it easy.

David (*relaxes on the floor*)   Gosh, you sure swing that wrench. Lots of times I do something and I wonder how they'd do it in the factory – you know, officially.

Gus   In the factory also they wonder sometimes how it's done officially.

David (*laughs*)   Yeh, I bet. (*Pause.* **Gus** *works.*) Gosh, I suddenly feel awful tired. I been at it all night, y'know?

Gus   Sleep, go ahead. I'll wake you when it gets interesting.

David   . . . Don't think you're doing this for nothing; I'll split the bill with you.

Gus   Nonsense. (*Laughs.*) We'll even it up sometime. One hand washes the other.

David's *head comes down on his arm, his face towards the Austrian. For several moments* **Gus** *works in silence.* **David**'s *breathing comes in longer draughts.* **Gus**, *noticing his eyes closed . . .*

Gus   Mr Beeves?

David *sleeps.*

Gus *comes out from under the car, gets his own coat and lays it over* **David** *and looks down at him. A smile comes to his face, he shakes his* *head wondrously, and looks from* **David** *all around the shop. Then, happily, and with a certain anticipation, he whispers . . .*

Gus   America!

He bends, slides under the car as the lights go down.

The lights come up on the same scene. From the large barn doors a wide shaft of sunlight is pouring in. **David** *is asleep where he was before, the coat still on him. But now the car is off the jack, and the hood is in place over the engine. The tools are in a neat pile nearby.*

Enter **JB**, **Dan Dibble**, **Hester**, **Pat** *and* **Amos**.

JB (*as they enter. To* **Dibble**)   We're a little early, so if he needs more time you'll wait, Dan . . . (*Looks at* **David**. *Quietly.*) What'd he do, sleep here all night?

Amos   Must've. He never come home.

JB (*to* **Dibble**)   That's the type of character you're dealing with. I hope you don't forget to thank him.

Dibble (*fearfully touching the fender*)   It looks just the same as when I brought it. You think it's fixed?

Hester *goes to* **David**.

JB (*looks at* **David**)   Don't worry, it's fixed.

Hester   Should I wake him?

JB   Go ahead. I want to tell him right away.

Hester (*bends over and shakes him lightly*)   Davey? Davey?

David   Huh?

Hester   Wake up. JB's here. It's morning. (*Laughs.*) Look at him!

David   Oh. (*Sits up and sees* **JB** *and* **Dibble**.) Oh ya, ya.

He gets up quickly, catching the coat as it falls from him. He looks at the coat for an instant.

JB   That's when you're young. Sleep anywhere. Nothin' bothers you.

David   What time is it?

JB   About half past ten.

David (*astonished and frightened*)   Half past ten! Gosh, I didn't mean to sleep that long . . . ! (*Looks around, suddenly anxious.*)

Hester (*laughs*)   You look so *funny*!

JB   Well, how'd you do, Dave, all finished?

David   Finished? Well, uh . . . (*He looks at the car.*)

JB   If you're not, Dan can wait.

David   Ya . . . just a second, I . . . (*He looks around the shop.*)

Hester   Looking for your tools? They're right on the floor here.

David (*he keeps looking all around for an instant. Looks at the tools*) Oh, okay. (*He looks at the car as though it were explosive. He lifts the hood and looks at the engine as . . .*)

JB   How was it, tough job?

David   Heh? Ya, pretty tough.

JB   Anything wrong . . . ?

David   No, I . . . (*He gets on his knees and looks under the engine.*)

Dibble   Can I start her up now?

David (*gets to his feet, looks at everyone as though in a dream*)   Okay, try her. Wait a minute, let me.

Dibble (*following him to the car door*)   Now don't dirty the upholstery . . .

JB   Don't worry about the upholstery, Dan, come over here.

Dibble (*coming to the front of car where* **JB** *and* **Hester** *are*) They always get in with their dirty clothes.

The engine starts. It hums smoothly, quietly. **JB** *turns proudly smiling to* **Dibble***: who creeps closer to it and listens.* **Hester** *watches* **JB**, *teetering on the edge of expectation, then watches* **Dibble***. After a* *moment the engine is shut off.* **David** *comes out of the car, comes slowly into view, his eyes wide.*

Pat (*to* **Dibble,** *of* **David**)   Highly skilled, highly skilled.

JB (*beaming, to* **Dibble**)   Well, you damn fool?

Dibble (*excitedly*)   Why, she does, she does sound fine. (*He snoops around the car.*)

David   Look, JB, I . . .

JB (*raises his fist and bangs on the fender*)   Goddam, Dave, I always said it! You know what you did?

Hester   Davey, JB's going to . . .

JB (*to* **Hester**)   I'm paying for it, at least let me tell it. Dan, come over here first and tell Dave what they did to you in Burley. Listen to this one, Dave. Pat, I want you to hear this.

Pat *and* **Amos** *come into the group.*

Dibble (*feeling the edge of the fender*)   I think he bumped it here.

JB   Oh, the hell with that, come over here and tell him. (**Dibble** *comes.*) What about that guy in Burley?

Dibble   Well, there's a garage in Burley does tractor work. But he's not reasonable . . .

JB   Tell him what he does.

Dibble   I brought this one to him and he says, 'I'll have to take her plumb apart, every screw and bolt of her.' He had his mind set on charging me a hundred and thirty-one dollars for the job. So, I figured it was just about time I stopped subsidisin' the Burley Garage Incorporated.

Pat   That's intelligent, Mr Dibble.

David   Did he tell you what was wrong with the car? The Burley man?

Dibble   Well, yes, he did, he always tells you something, but I can't . . . Now wait a minute . . . These things have a dingus they call a . . . a crankshaft? He said it was crooked, or busted, or dented . . .

JB (*laughs – to* **David**, *then back to* **Dibble**)   On a brand new Marmon! What the hell did he want with the crankshaft?

Pat   Scandalous.

David   Look, JB, lemme tell you . . .

JB (*drawing* **David** *and* **Dibble** *together*)   Go ahead, David. And listen to this, Dan. This is the first honest word you ever heard out of a mechanic. (*To* **David**.) Go on, tell this poor sucker what the matter was.

David *stands dumbly, looking into* **JB**'s *ecstatic face. He turns to* **Hester**.

Hester (*hardly able to stand still. Pridefully*)   Tell him, Davey!

David (*turns back to* **JB**. *He sighs*)   Just a lot of small things, that's all.

David *walks a few steps away to a fender and absently touches it. It could be taken for modesty.* **Amos** *is now to the side, resting a foot on the car bumper – watching in wonder.*

JB   Well? What do you say, Danny? Now you're looking at a *mechanic*!

Pat (*to* **Dibble**, *of* **David**)   At the age of six he fixed the plug on an iron.

Dibble (*goes to* **David**)   Look, David. I have a proposition for you. Whenever there's a job to do on my tractors charge me for parts and that's all. If you'd do that for me, I could guarantee you more.

David   I'm much obliged to you, Mr Dibble, but I'm not tooled up for tractor work.

JB   Now wait a minute . . .

David (*almost shouting with tension*)   Let me say something, will you? To work on heavy engines like that, and tractors in general, a man has got to be a . . . well, I'm not tooled up for it, that's all, I haven't got the machinery.

JB (*businesslike*)   But you've got the machinery.

Hester   Listen to this, Davey!

David *looks at him.*

JB   You go out and buy everything you want. Fix up this building. Lay out a concrete driveway in the front. I'll pay the bills. Give me one per cent on my money. (*Roundly.*) Let me be some good in my life!

David (*as though a fever were rising in him, his voice begins to soar*) I don't know if I'm ready for that, JB . . . I'd have to study about tractors . . . I . . .

JB   Then study! Now's the *time*, Dave. You're young, strong . . . !

Pat (*to* **Dibble**)   He's very strong.

Dibble (*taking out a roll*)   How much do I owe you, boy?

David *looks at* **Dibble**.

David   Owe me?

JB   Make it sixty dollars flat, Dave. Since it wasn't as hard as we thought. (**David** *looks at* **JB** *who won't wait for him to object.*) Sixty flat, Dan.

Dibble (*counts laboriously, peeling off each bill into* **David**'s *unwilling hand*)   One, two, three . . . (*Continues.*)

Hester (*joyously amused at* **Dibble**)   What're those, all ones?!

Dibble   All I carry is ones. Never can tell when you'll leave a five by mistake. (*Continues counting*) Government ought to print different sizes.

JB   How's it feel to have two stars, heh, Pat? (*With a sweep of his hand.*) I can see a big red sign out there way up in the air. Dave Beeves, Incorporated, Tractor Station . . .

Hester *has noticed the coat beside car.*

Hester (*holding the coat up*)   Did you get a new coat?

Dibble *continues counting into* **David***'s hand.*

Hester   Huh?

Quickly turns to **Hester** *and the coat.* **Dibble** *continues counting.* **David** *stares at the coat, suddenly in the full blast of all the facts. Now all but* **Dibble** *are looking at the coat.*

Amos (*feels the coat*)   Where'd you get this?

Dibble   Hold still! Fifty-three, fifty-four, fifty . . .

David *looks at* **Amos***, then down at his hand into which the money is still dropping. He then looks again at* **Amos** *. . .* **Amos** *to him.*

Amos   What's the matter?

Hester   What's come over you?

David *suddenly hands the money to* **Hester***.*

Dibble   Say!

David (*his hand recedes from the bills as though they were burning. To* **Hester**)   Take it, will ya? I . . .

He starts to point somewhere off right as though he were being called. Then his hand drops . . . and with gathering speed he strides out.

Hester (*astonished*)   Davey . . . (*She hurries to watch him leaving, to the right, halts.*) Why . . . he's running! (*Calling in alarm.*) Davey! (*She runs out.*)

JB, **Pat** *and* **Dibble** *stand, watching them open-mouthed, as they disappear down the driveway.* **Amos** *is centre, downstage.*

Dibble   What in the world come over the boy? I didn't finish payin' him.

They stand looking right. **Amos** *looks at the coat. He starts turning it inside out, examining it carefully, perplexed.*

Slow curtain.

Act Two

Scene One

June. Three years later. The living room of the Falks' – now David's – house. A farmhouse room, but brightly done over. Solid door to outside at the right. In the back wall, right, a swinging door to the dining room. A stairway at the back, its landing at the left. A door, leading to an office in the bedroom, down left. One window at left. Two windows flanking the door to outside at right. Good blue rug, odd pieces, some new, some old. Oak. A pair of well-used rubber boots beside the door.

The stage is empty. A perfect summer day, not too hot. Noon. After a moment the doorbell rings.

Hester (*from above, shouts excitedly*)   They're here! Davey!

David (*hurrying down the stairs, buttoning on a white shirt. He wears pressed pants, shined shoes, his hair has just been combed; shouting up*) I'll get it, I'm going!

Hester (*her head sticking out at the junction of banister and ceiling. She quickly surveys the room as* **David** *comes off the stairs*)   Get your boots out of there! I just fixed up the house!

The bell rings.

David (*calling towards the door*)   Just a minute! (*Getting the boots together. To* **Hester**.) Go on, get dressed, it's almost noon! (*He opens door to dining room.*)

Hester   Don't put them in there! They're filthy! Down the cellar!

David   But I always put them in here!

Hester   But you promised once the house is painted!

Door opens. Enter **Gus**.

Gus   Don't bother. It's only me.

He wears a white Palm Beach suit, hatless. **Hester** *and* **David** *stare at him in astonishment. She comes down the stairs. She is dressed in a robe, but has her best shoes on. Her hair is set.*

Hester   Why, Gus! You look so handsome!

Gus   It is such a special day, I decided to make an impression on myself.

Hester   No, you go perfectly with the room.

David (*laughing with* **Gus**)   Watch yourself or she'll hang you in a frame over the couch. (*He stamps at her to get her moving.*)

Hester (*squealing, she runs to the stairs and up a few steps, and leans over the banister*)   Is your girl outside? Bring her in.

David   Hey, that's right! Where's your girl?

Gus (*looking up*)   Well, we both decided suddenly that until she can become as beautiful as Hester . . .

Hester   Oh, you.

Gus (*opening his arms like a pleading lover*)   Until she shows ability to make over a house like this was, and until etcetera and etcetera, she is not the girl for me, so I haven't seen her all week. Anyway, I have decided definitely I need only a red-headed girl.

Hester (*to* **Gus**)   Stand in the middle of the room when they come in. You make it look just like the picture in the *Ladies Home Journal*.

David (*starting after her*)   Get dressed, will ya? Dad'll cut my head off if we're not ready!

Hester *laughs with delight and runs upstairs.*

Gus (*looking around*)   It came out so nice. You know, this house shines in the sun a quarter of a mile away.

David   Well, look at that sun! (*Goes right to windows.*) God must've pulled up the sun this morning, grabbed him by the back of the neck, and said – make it a baseball day.

Gus (*touching the wall*)   Now it is truly a place to call home.
Amazing.

David (*laughs musingly, indicating the windows at the right*)   You
know, when I came down this morning that window caught
my eye. I used to sneak under that window when we were kids
and peek in here to watch Hester doing her homework. And
then I used to sneak away. And now I can walk in and outa
this house fifty times a day and sleep up in his room night after
night! (*Looks through the window.*) Wherever he is I bet he still
can't figure it out. Read the encyclopaedia if you like. I'll put
on a tie. (*Goes to the landing.*)

Gus (*looking around*)   Encyclopaedia, furniture, new plumbing . . .
When am I going to see a couple of brats around here!

David (*stops at the landing*)   What's the rush, you got some old
suits you want ruined?

Gus   Me? I always pick up babies by the back of the neck,
but . . . (*Idly.*) Without children you wouldn't have to fix nothin'
in here for twenty years. When nothing breaks, it's boring. (*He
sits, reaches over for an encyclopaedia volume.*)

David (*glances above, comes away from stairs. Quietly*)   I been
wanting to ask you about that.

Gus   What?

David (*hesitates. In good humour*)   Did you ever hear of it
happening when people didn't have kids because of the man?

Gus   Certainly, why not? Why don't you talk it over with her?

David (*laughs self-consciously*)   I can't seem to get around to it.
I mean, we somehow always took it for granted, kinda, that
when the time was right a kid would just naturally come along.

Gus   You go to the doctor, then you'll know . . . Or do you
want to know?

David   Sure I do, but I don't know, it just doesn't seem *right*,
especially when we've been all set financially for over two years
now.

Gus   Right! What has this got to do with right or wrong? There is no justice in the world.

David (*looks at him, then goes to the landing, stops*)   I'll never believe that, Gus. If one way or another a man don't receive according to what he deserves inside . . . well, it's a madhouse.

Hester (*from above*)   There's a car stopping in front of the house! (*Coming down.*) Did you put your boots away?

David (*slightly annoyed*)   Yeh, I put 'em away! (*Goes across to the door.*)

Hester (*hurrying downstairs*)   You didn't! (*Hurrying across the room towards the boots.*) He'll have the place like a pigsty in a week!

David *opens the door and looks out.*

Gus (*to **Hester***)   Get used to it, the place will never be so neat once you have children around.

David *turns to him, quickly, resentment in his face.*

Hester (*stops moving. An eager glow lights up her expression. The boots are in her hand*)   Don't you think it is a wonderful house for children?

David   Hello! Hello, Mr Dibble! Didn't expect to see you around here today. Come in, come in.

*Enter **Dan Dibble** after wiping his feet carefully on the doormat.*

Dibble   Had to see JB on some business. Thought I'd stop in, say hello. Afternoon, Mrs Beeves.

Hester   Hello, Mr Dibble. (*She picks up the boots and goes out.*)

David   You know Gus Eberson. He's with me over at the shop.

Dibble   Sure, how are you, Gus? Say, you look more like a banker than a mechanic.

David   Best mechanic there is.

Dibble   What I always say – never judge a man by his clothes. A man and his clothes are soon parted. (*They laugh.*)

Say, JB was tellin' me you used to have a shop of your own
here in town – over in Poplar Street, was it . . . ?

David   We amalgamated, Gus and I.

Gus   Actually, Mr Dibble, I ran out of money and customers
after the first seven months. I am working now for Mr Beeves
since over two years.

Dibble   Well, say, this is the first time I knew a hired man to
insist he wasn't the boss's partner, and the boss to let on he was.

Gus (*chuckles*)   Mr Beeves suffers sometimes from an over-
developed sense of responsibility.

Dibble   That's why I spotted him as a natural mink man.
Given it any more thought, David?

David   A lot, Mr Dibble, a lot – but I'm afraid I haven't got
an answer for you yet.

Dibble   Got time for a few facts today?

David   Tell you the truth, we're expecting JB and Shory.
Goin' up to Burley for the ball game. You heard about my
brother, didn't you?

Dibble   JB said somethin' about him pitchin' against that
coloured team. Say, if he can knock them boys over he really
belongs in the big leagues.

David   I guess after today's game Amos Beeves will be playin'
for the Detroit Tigers.

Dibble   Well, say, they really took him, eh?

David   Just about. A Tiger scout's goin' to be in the
grandstand today.

Dibble   Well, say, it's about time.

David   Yep, things even up, I guess, in the long run. Why
don't you drop around tonight? Havin' a big barbecue after
the game.

Enter **Hester** *from dining room.*

Dibble   Thanks, I'd like to but I got to get back and see my mink get fed on time and proper.

Hester   David just never stops talkin' about mink. (*Sits.*) Have you still got that tiny one with the white spot on his head?

David (*seeing* **Hester**'s *interest, kindles a happy liveliness in him*) Oh, that one's probably been in and out of a dozen New York night clubs by this time. (*They laugh.*)

Hester (*disturbed – to* **Dibble**)   Oh, you didn't kill her?

David (*to* **Gus** *and* **Hester**)   That's the way you get about mink, they're like people, little nervous people.

Dibble   I call them my little bankers myself. Pour a dollar's worth of feed down their gullets and they'll return you forty per cent; best little bankers in the world.

David   Except when they fall, Mr Dibble, except when they fall.

Dibble   Mink never fall!

David   Oh, now, Mr Dibble . . .

Dibble   They don't! It's their keepers fall down on them. When a feller goes broke tryin' to raise mink, it's mainly because he's a careless man. From everything I've seen, David, you ain't that kind. You got a farm here clean as a hospital and mink needs a clean place. You're the first and only man I thought of when I decided to sell off some of my breeders when my doctor told me to ease up.

David   I been askin' around lately, and everybody I talked to . . .

Dibble (*to* **Gus** *too*)   I'm glad you made the inquiries. It shows you're a careful man. And now I'll tell you my answer. Easiest thing in the world is to kill a mink. Mink'll die of a cold draught; they'll die of heart failure; indigestion can kill them, a cut lip, a bad tooth or sex trouble. And worse than that, the mink is a temperamental old woman. I wear an old brown

canvas coat when I work around them. If I change that coat
it might start them to eating their young. A big loud noise like
thunder, or a heavy hailstorm comes and the mother's liable to
pick up the litter, put 'em out in the open part of the cage, and
then she'll go back into the nest box and close her eyes. As
though they're out of danger if they're out of her sight. And
when the storm's over you might have six or eight kits drowned
to death out there. I've seen mink murder each other, I've seen
them eat themselves to death and starve themselves to death,
and I've seen them die of just plain worry. But! Not on my
ranch! I'll show my records to anybody.

David (*to* **Gus**)   There's a business, boy!

Gus   A business! That's a slot machine. What do you need
with mink?

David   Oh, there's a kick in it, Gus. When you send a load
of skins to New York you know you *did* something, you . . .

Gus   Why, you didn't do something? (*Indicates right.*) A great
big shop you built up, a tractor station, how nice you made this
farm . . . ?

David (*not too intensely; he enjoys this talk*)   Yeh, but is a thing
really yours because your name is on it? Don't you have to feel
you're smart enough, or strong enough, or something enough
to have won it before it's really yours? You can't bluff a mink
into staying alive. (*Turns to* **Dibble**.) I tell you, Mr Dibble . . .

Dibble   Take your time. Think about it.

David   Let me call you. I'll let you know,

Dibble   Oh, I'll bide my time. Just remember, in New York
they murder people for a mink coat. Women sell their jewels
for mink, they sell their . . . them New York women'll sell
damn near anything for mink!

They laugh, as horns of two cars sound urgently outside.

David (*to* **Dibble**)   This is my brother!

Gus (*as* **David** *opens the door*)   Look, like two peacocks!

Hester (*at the door, over her shoulder ecstatically to* **Dibble**)   They've waited so long!

David (*exuberantly, backing from the door*)   Here he comes! Christy Matthewson the Second!

Enter **Amos** *and* **Pat***, followed by* **JB**.

Hester (*grabbing* **Amos***'s hand*)   How's your arm, Ame!

Amos (*winds up and pitches*)   Wham! – He's out!

Pat (*throwing up his arms*)   God bless this day! (*Suddenly.*) I'm not waiting for anybody! (*Threatens to go out again.*)

JB (*to* **Hester**)   Shory's waiting in the car! Let's go!

Hester   Bring him in. Let's have a drink!

Nobody hears her.

David   What're you lookin' so sad about, Dad? (*Suddenly hugs* **Pat***.*)

Hester   Get some whisky, Dave!

Pat (*indignantly – he has broken from* **David**)   You want to suffocate in here? Open the windows in this house! (*He rushes around throwing windows up.*)

David (*laughing*)   We're going in a minute! Where's the telegram, Ame! (**Amos** *opens his mouth but* **Pat** *cuts him off.*)

Pat (*busy with the windows*)   Let the day come in! What a day! What a year! What a nation!

Hester (*rushing after* **Pat**)   Did you bring the telegram? (*She corners him, laughing.*) Where's the telegram?

Pat   I don't need to bring it. I will never forget that telegram so long as I live. (*Takes it out of his pocket.*) 'Western Union. Class of Service. This is a full-rate Telegram or Cablegram unless its deferred character is indicated by a suitable symbol . . . '

Hester   What're you reading that part for? (*Tries to grab it from him.*) What did the scout say?!

Pat (*grabbing it back*)   I'm reading it to you just the way I read it when I got it – from the very top, to the very bottom.

David   Let him read it, Hess!

They go quiet.

Pat   I haven't felt this way since the last time I read the Bible. 'Patterson Beeves, 26 Murdock Street. Will be in Burley for the Black Giants game Sunday, July 16th. Looking forward to seeing Amos Beeves's performance. Best regards, Augie Belfast, Detroit Tigers.' (*Looks around imperiously.*) Twenty-one years I have been waiting for this telegram. Training him down the cellar since he was old enough to walk. People laughed when Amos got bad marks in school. Forget the homework, I said. Keep your eye on the ball. Concentration, I said . . .

JB (*touched and fearing* **Pat***'s continuing indefinitely*)   For God's sake, let's all have a drink!

David   Comin' up! (*Goes out door.*)

Hester (*pointing outside. To* **JB**)   I'll bring Ellie in! Why don't you come to the game with us, Mr Dibble? (*She starts across to the door.*)

JB (*a little embarrassed, stops* **Hester**)   Better leave her, baby. You know how she is about alcohol. Let's not start anything.

Gus   Shory likes a drink. I'll bring him in. (*He goes out left.*)

Pat   Plenty of room in Dave's car, Mr Dibble. (*He studies* **Dibble***, automatically massaging* **Amos***'s arm.*)

JB (*holds his hand out to* **Hester**)   What do you think of this?

Hester   A wedding ring! You giving Ellie a new ring?

JB (*warmly*)   No, this is for me. Since we decided to adopt a baby I been feeling like we're newlyweds.

Hester (*flings her arms around him*)   You're such a silly man!

Enter **Shory***, pushed in by* **Gus***.*

Shory (*to* **JB**)   Hey, Poppa, don't start nothin' you can't finish.

*Enter **David** with drinks on a tray.*

Hester (*three-quarters joking, but only that much. To **Shory***)   And you've got a filthy mind.

Shory   Madam, don't flatter me. (*To **David**, who has been watching **Hester** since **Shory** came in.*) Hey, husband, where's that drink?

David   Come on, everybody. Before we go! (*Gives out the drinks . . . Raises his glass.*) A toast! To everybody's luck – everybody's!

All raise their glasses.

Gus (*to **Amos***)   And the next World's Series! (*Starts to drink.*)

David   Wait! Make one big toast . . . to all our hearts' desires. For Amos! For Dad.

Gus   To David and Hester! To their prosperity, their shop, their tractor station, their farm.

Dibble (*suddenly struck with the idea*)   And their mink!

Hester (*quick complaint*)   No.

David (*he looks at **Hester**. Her face softens towards him*)   Not the mink now! From today on everything is coming true! To our children.

Gus   To their children.

JB   Their children.

Hester (*softly*)   And in this year. Say that.

David (*their eyes meet for an instant, and hold*)   In this year everything our hearts desire . . . *all of us*: in this year.

All drink.

Pat (*looks at watch*)   Hey! We're late! We're getting drunk and the whole world is waiting for us out there! Come on!

They all rush out yelling and laughing as . . .

Curtain.

Scene Two

Living room. About seven o'clock that night.

The stage is empty. The gentle murmur and occasional laughter of the guests at the barbecue can be heard dimly. Presently, **David**, *followed by* **Dan Dibble**, *come in through the front door.* **David** *crosses to the desk and removes a large cheque book. He pauses over it, pen in hand.*

David   It's a fortune. I never wrote a cheque this big in my life.

Dibble   You never got so much for so little, David. You'll have prize stock, the finest breeding mink alive. The rest's up to you.

David   Mr Dibble, I never thought I'd see my hand shaking.

The door at lower left opens and **Pat** *appears. He closes the door gently behind him.*

David   Still asleep?

Pat   Shhh. I always make him take a long nap after a game.

David   Aren't you going to eat anything?

Pat   I couldn't eat anything now. I'll eat after Belfast gets here. (*He sits on the couch.*) I was watchin' Amos just now asleep on the couch, and it suddenly struck me. Did you ever notice what a powerful face he has?

David (*as he writes cheque*)   He's great. After that game today there ain't a man in the world can doubt it. He's just great.

Pat   Didn't he look noble out there?

David   Noble enough to vote for.

David (*as he tears out cheque*)   Here's your cheque, Mr Dibble. (**Dibble** *takes it.*)

Dibble   You'll never regret it, David.

David   I hope not.

Dibble   Well, I'll be runnin' along now. You call me as soon as you get your cages ready and I'll bring 'em over. (**David** *has walked him to the front door.*) Goodnight.

David   G'night.

Dibble *exits.* **David** *turns back into the room.*

Pat   You know why I'm extra glad? I think you were beginning to take it too hard, Dave. I was going to have a talk with you. Because I never had a doubt he'd scale the heights.

David   I just didn't like the idea of me getting everything so steady, and him waiting around like . . . I mean, you get to wondering if your own turn isn't coming.

Pat   Like what do you mean?

David   A loss . . . a big unhappiness of some kind. But he's on his way now. I know it, Pop.

The door opens and **JB** *enters with a brand new valise. He is slightly drunk. In one hand he has a slip of paper.*

JB   Surprise! (**Pat** *springs up with finger to his lips.*)

Pat   Shhh!

JB *(whispers)*   Surprise! Wake him up. (*Pointing to valise.*) Surprise . . .

Pat   After a game he's got to sleep an hour or he's peevish. (*Pointing at watch.*) Wait a few minutes.

David   Wait'll he sees the initials.

Pat *(violently)*   Sssh! (*To* **JB** . . . *threatening*) If he's peevish . . . !

The door opens and **Amos** *stands in the doorway.*

JB   Hey, Amos . . . (*Holding up valise.*) Surprise.

Amos   Aw . . . ! (**Amos** *takes the valise and fingers it happily.*)

JB   It's a token of our affection from . . . just a minute now . . . (*Straightens the slip of paper.*) Hester, Shory, Gus, Dave, Ellie, and me, and Belle. (*Indicating upstage.*)

Amos *(fondling the valise)*   Gee, you should'na done it.

JB (*with growing flourish and sentiment*)   No, you don't realise the travelling you'll do. (*Looks into the distance.*) Shibe Park, Commiskey Field, Sportsman's Park – Boston, Chicago, Cleveland, St Louis . . . And when you're packing up after a nice no-hitter, you'll give us a thought in the old home town. (*To clinch it, he taps a buckle.*) Solid brass.

Amos (*feverish in glory, he gets up*)   Give me that list. (*Takes it out of* **JB**'s *hand.*) When I get my first pay-cheque I'm gonna send you all a big present! Say . . . ! (*Starting to take* **Pat**'s *wrist to look at his watch.*) What time . . . ?

Pat (*holding onto his arm*)   You heard what he said in the locker room. He's got to finish some long-distance phoning, and then he'll be here. Come on. I'll rub you down.

Hester *enters as they start for the stairs.*

Hester   John, you better go outside. Ellie's going home.

JB (*frightened and hurt*)   Why? (*To all.*) Am I so drunk?

David   Hurry up, maybe you can catch her.

JB   Come with me, Dave . . . tell her.

David   Get washed, Ame . . . you want to look nice now. Be right back.

David *and* **JB** *go out.*

Hester (*looking at the door*)   Why must he always do that? (*To* **Pat** *who is rummaging in his old valise.*) I'll get you some towels. Come on up.

Pat   Oh, no, we carry our own. You never can tell about strange towels. (*He folds one over his arm.* **Amos** *is looking out of the window.*)

Hester (*ready to laugh*)   Well, I wasn't going to give you a dirty towel, you stupid.

Pat   For twenty-one years I've kept him practically sterilised. I ain't layin' him low with an infection now. Come on, Amos, get washed.

Amos and **Pat** *exit up the stairs as* **JB** *enters, followed by* **David**.
JB *is drunk, unsteady but not staggering. He barges in, comes directly
to* **Hester** *and takes her hand, speaks very close to her face, as though to
discern her reactions better.*

JB   Hester, you got to go home for me. (*He goes to window
helplessly.*)

David   Maybe she was only fooling, John . . .

JB   No! But . . . (*To* **Hester**.) Somebody's got to go home for
me! (*And suddenly he bursts into uncontrolled sobbings.*)

Hester   What in the world . . .

David (*angrily*)   John! (*Shakes him, then seats him.*) John! Are you
going to cut that out?

Hester (*going to* **JB**)   What happened? What did she say?

JB (*stops sobbing, sits swaying backwards, and forwards, very slightly in
his chair*)   All these years . . . we could've had children . . . all
these weary, weary years.

Hester   What are you talking about?

JB (*pointing waywardly towards the door to the outside*)   Just told
me . . . she made it up about the doctor . . . made it all up. We
could've had two kids by now. (*Looks at* **David**.) She wouldn't.
She wouldn't. Because I drink, she says. A drunkard, she says!
They'll wipe my name off my mail box like I never lived!

Hester   Come upstairs and lie down. You make me so mad
I could choke you! You could have everything in the world and
you drink it away.

JB   If I had a boy . . . I wouldn't have touched a drop.

Hester   Oh, push! (*She tries to move him to the stairway.*)

JB   I'm only a failure, Dave. The world is full of failures. All
a man needs is one mistake and he's a failure.

David *turns his head, a little annoyed.*

David (*impatiently*)   I know, John. (*Looks out window again.*)

JB You are the only man I ever knew who never makes a mistake. You understand me. Look at me! I am saying something.

David (*now turns full to him*)   What are you talking about?

JB I'm not as drunk as I look, David! You're a good man, yes. You know how to do. But you've had a phenomenal lot of luck in your life, Dave. Never play luck too hard. It's like a season, and seasons pass away.

Hester Come up or you'll pass away.

Enter **Pat** *downstairs with watch in hand.*

Pat My watch says eight-thirty, where is he? He told you no later than eight o'clock, didn't he?

David Which means he's half an hour late. That's what it means, doesn't it?

Pat I don't know what to tell Amos. I made him take another shower.

David (*with growing fear*)   He pitched the greatest game of his life today, what more does he need to be told? That man'll be here.

Pat Maybe he was kidding us. He looked like he might be that type.

David Are you going to stop that?

Pat . . . And Amos did look a little nervous in the eighth inning with those two men on base.

David But they didn't score! Now will you just stop.

Pat, *hurt, looks at him, then goes to the stairs.*

David Dad, what you want me to do; I can't grow him in my back yard, can I?

Shory *enters, pushed by* **Gus**. *At the stairs,* **Pat** *turns, starts to speak, then goes up and out.*

Shory (*as the door shuts*)   I'm getting my aches and pains. I came in to say goodnight . . . Party's breakin' up anyway out there.

David   No, wait a little. I don't want everybody pulling out.

He goes to window as . . .

Shory   The man told you seven-thirty, what're you making believe he said eight? You told me as he said seven-thirty, didn't you?

David (*his fury is at the scout. He keeps searching out of the window*) He could've got a flat maybe.

Shory   It don't take an hour to change a flat, Dave.

David (*tensely. He turns*)   Don't go away. Please.

Enter **Hester**.

David (*to* **Hester**)   The folks are starting to go. (*Moving her back to the door.*) I want a party here when the scout leaves. Keep them here.

Hester   It's not the world coming to an end. I don't want you acting this way. It's no fault of yours what happens to him. (*She grasps him.*) Why do you act this way? Davey . . .

David   I don't get it, I swear to God I don't get it. (*Strides to the window. He seems about to burst from the room.*)

Shory   Get what?

David   Everything is so hard for him. (*Turns to them suddenly, unable to down his anxiety.*) I want to ask you something. All of you, and you too, Hess. You know what I can do and what I can't do, you . . . you know me. Everything I touch, why is it? It turns gold. Everything.

Hester   What's come over you? Why . . . ?

David (*with extreme urgency*)   It bothers me, it . . . (*To all.*) What is it about me? I never . . . I never lose. Since we were kids I expected Amos to rise and shine. He's the one, he knows something, he knows one thing perfect. Why? Is it all luck? Is that what it is?

Gus   Nonsense. You're a good man, David.

David   Aren't you good?

Gus   Yes, but I . . .

David   Then why did your shop fail? Why are you working for me now? (*He moves as one in the throes of release.*)

Gus   They remember the war here, Dave, they don't like to buy from a foreigner.

David   No, that's crazy.

Gus   Also, I had a second-rate location.

David   Gus, it was better than mine. Every car coming into town had to pass your place. And they came to me. Why is that?

Gus   You know an engine, Dave, you . . .

David   Including Marmons? (*To all.*) I got fourteen thousand dollars in the bank and as much again standing on the ground. Amos? Never had a nickel. Not a bloody nickel. Why?

A slight pause.

Hester (*goes to him. Smiles to make him smile but he does not*)   Why does it bother you? It's good to be lucky. Isn't it?

David (*looks at her a moment*)   Isn't it better to feel that what you have came to you because of something special you can do? Something, something . . . inside you? Don't you have to know what that thing is?

Hester   Don't you know?

David   . . . I don't, I don't know.

Shory   And you'll never know.

David   Damn it all, if everything drops on you like fruit from a tree, for no reason, why can't it break away for no reason? Everything you have . . . suddenly.

Hester (*takes **David**'s arm*)   Come, say goodbye to the folks.

David   No . . . they're not going home till the scout comes! Now go out.

Hester (*shakes his arm*)   It's his hard luck, not yours!

David   It is mine! A man has a right to get what he deserves. He does, damn it! (*He goes to the window, breaking from her.*)

Hester (*angrily*)   You talk like you'd stole something from him. You never got anything you didn't deserve. You . . .

David (*at the end of his patience, he turns on her*)   Am I that good and he that bad? I can't believe it. There's something wrong, there's something wrong! (*Suddenly.*) I'm going to Burley. (*To* **Hester**, *hurriedly.*) Where's the keys to the car . . . ?

Hester   You don't even know where to find the man . . .

David   I'll find him, where are the keys?

Hester (*she grabs him*)   Davey, stop it.

David   I'm going, I'll drag him here.

Hester (*fright*)   Davey . . .

He strides towards the door. **Shory** *grabs his arm and holds it fast.*

Shory   Stop it!

David   Let go of me!

Shory (*he will not let go*)   Listen to me, you damn fool! There's nothing you can do, you understand?

David   Let go of my arm.

Shory (*forces him down into a chair*)   David, I'm going to tell you something . . . I never told you before. But you need to know this now. Amos deserves better than this, but I deserved better than this too. (*Pats his thighs.*) When I went to France there was no broken bones in my imagination. I left this town with a beautiful moustache and full head of hair. Women travelled half the state to climb into my bed. Even over there, under shot and shell, as they say, there was a special star over my head. I was the guy nothin' was ever going to hit . . . And nothin' ever did, David. (*He releases* **David**'s *arm. Now* **David** *does not move away.*) Right through the war without a scratch.

Surprised? I walked into Paris combing my hair. The women were smiling at me from both sides of the street, and I walked up the stairs with the whistles blowing out the Armistice. I remember how she took off my shoes and put them under the bed. The next thing I knew the house was laying on my chest and they were digging me out.

David, *all, stare at him.*

Hester   Everybody said it was a battle, I thought . . .

Shory (*to her*)   No, no battle at all. (*To* **David**.) In battle – there's almost a reason for it, a man almost 'deserves' it that way. I just happened to pick out the one woman in Paris who lived in a house where the janitor was out getting drunk on the Armistice. He forgot to put water in the furnace boiler. (*Smiles.*) The walls blew out. (*Points upstage with his thumb over his shoulder.*) Amos's walls happened to blow out. And you happen to be a lucky boy, brother David. A jellyfish can't swim no matter how he tries; it's the tide that pushes him every time. So just keep feeding, and enjoy the water till you're thrown up on the beach to dry.

Pause.

Hester (*goes to him*)   Come, Dave, the folks are waiting to say goodbye.

David *is forced to turn quickly towards the window. It is an indecisive turn of the head, a questioning turn, and she follows as he strides to the window and looks out towards upstage direction . . .*

David   Wait! (*Starting for the window.*) A car? (*Turns quickly to them all.*) It didn't go past. It stopped. (*He starts quickly for the door, across the stage, right.* **Pat** *rushes down the stairs.*)

Pat   He's here! He came! Get out, everybody! (*To all.*) All the way from Burley in a taxicab! Dave, you stay. I want your advice when he starts talkin' contract! (**Pat** *rushes out.*)

David (*as they all keep exclaiming*)   Out, out, all of you! (*As they start for door,* **David** *musses* **Shory**.) Where's your jellyfish now, brother?!

Shory (*at door with the others*)   His luck is with him, sister, that's all, his luck!

David   Luck, heh? (*Smiling, he bends over* **Shory**, *pointing left towards his big desk and speaking privately* . . .) Some day remind me to open the middle drawer of that desk. I'll show you a fistful of phone bills for calls to Detroit.

Gus (*joyously*)   Dave. You called them!

David   Sure, I called them. That man is here because I brought him here! (*To* **Shory**.) Where's the jellyfish could've done that! (*Triumphantly, to all.*) Don't anybody go. We're going to raise the roof tonight!

They have all gone out now, on his last lines. Only **Hester** *remains in the doorway.* **David** *looks at her a moment, and with a laugh embraces her quickly.*

David   I'll tell you everything he says.

Hester   Be like this all the time, Davey. (*She turns towards the hallway into which this door leads.*) Tell me every word, now. (*She goes.*)

David *quickly brushes his hair back, looking rapidly about the room and to himself.*

David   Now it's wonderful: This is how it ought to be!

Enter **Amos** – *comes downstairs.*

Amos (*hushed, with his hands clasped as though in prayer*)   God, it's happening just like it ought've. 'Cause I'm good. I betcha I'm probably great! (*He says this, facing the door, glancing at* **David**.)

Enter **Augie Belfast** *and* **Pat**. **Augie** *is a big Irishman, dressed nattily.*

Pat (*as they enter*)   . . . couldn't stop him from setting up a party. (*Sees* **David**.) Oh, here he is.

Augie (*to* **Amos** *and* **David**)   Sit down, sit down. Don't stand on ceremony with me. I'm Augie Belfast . . .

Amos *sits on the bed.* **David** *in a chair. As* **Pat** . . .

Pat   Let me have your coat?

Augie (*lays down his hat*)   It don't bother me. I live in it.
Thanks just the same. (*Taking out chewing gum.*) Gum?

David   No thanks, we've been eating all day . . . mean . . .

Augie (*unfolding a slice as* **Pat** *sits. He moves about constantly; he
already has a wad of gum in his cheek*)   Loosen up, don't stand
in awe of me. (*To* **David** *and* **Amos**.) I was just telling your
father . . . I got tied up in Burley on some long-distance calls.
I'm very sorry to be so late. (*He is anxious to be pardoned.*)

David   Oh, that's all right. We know how busy you fellas are.

Augie   Thanks. I knew how you must've been feeling. (*He
paces a little, chewing, looking at the floor.*) Amos? (*He says nothing for
a long moment. Stops walking, looks down, slowly unfolds another slice
of gum.*)

Amos (*whisper*)   Ya?

Augie   Amos, how long you been pitchin'?

Amos   Well, about . . . (*Turns to* **Pat**.)

Pat   Steadily since he's been nine years old.

Augie (*nods. Pause*)   I guess you know he's a damn fine pitcher.

Pat (*comfortably*)   We like to think so around here.

Augie   Yeh, he's steady, he's good. Got a nice long arm, no
nerves in that arm. He's all right. He feels the plate. (*All the time
thinking of something else, pacing.*)

Pat   Well, you see, I've had him practising down the cellar
against a target. Dug the cellar out deeper so he could have
room after he grew so tall.

Augie   Yeh, I know. Man sitting next to me this afternoon
was telling me. Look, Mr Beeves . . . (*He straddles a chair, folds his
arms on its back, facing them.*) I want you to have confidence in
what I say. I'm Augie Belfast, if you know anything about
Augie Belfast you know he don't bull. There's enough
heartbreak in this business without bull-throwers causin' any

more. *In toto*, I don't string an athlete along. Pitchin' a baseball to me is like playin' the piano well, or writin' beautiful literature, so try to feel I'm giving you the last word because I am. (**Pat** *nods a little, hardly breathing.*) I have watched many thousands of boys, Mr Beeves. I been whackin' the bushes for material for a long time. You done a fine job on Amos. He's got a fine, fast ball, he's got a curve that breaks off sharp, he's got his control down to a pinpoint. He's almost original sometimes. When it comes to throwin' a ball, he's all there. Now. (*Slight pause.*) When I saw him two years ago, I said . . .

David (*electrically*)   You were *here* before?

Augie   Oh yeh, I meant to tell you. I came to see him last year, too . . .

Pat   Why didn't you let me know?

Augie   Because there was one thing I couldn't understand, Mr Beeves. I understand it today, but I couldn't then. When the bases are clear, Mr Beeves, and there's nobody on, your boy is terrific . . . Now wait a minute, let me say rather that he's good, very good . . . I don't want to say an untruth, your boy is good when nobody's on. But as soon as a man gets on base and starts rubbin' his spikes in the dirt and makin' noise behind your boy's back, something happens to him. I seen it once, I seen it twice. I seen it every time the bases get loaded. And once the crowd starts howlin', your boy, Mr Beeves, is floatin' somewhere out in paradise.

Pat   But he pitched a shut-out.

Augie   Only because them Black Giants like to swing bats. If they'd waited him out in the eighth inning they could've walked in half a dozen runs. Your boy was out of control. (*Dead silence.*) I couldn't understand it. I absolutely couldn't get the angle on it. Here's a boy with a terrific . . . Well, let's not say terrific, let's say a damn good long arm. But not an ounce of base-brains. There is something in him that prevents him from playin' the bases.

Pat   I know, I've been drilling him the last three years.

Augie   I know, but in three years there's been no improvement. In fact, this year he's worse in that respect than last year. Why? Today I found the answer.

Pat (*softly*)   You did?

Augie   The guy sitting next to me mentions about him pitchin' down the cellar since he was nine years old. That was it! Follow me now. In the cellar there is no crowd. In the cellar he knows exactly what's behind his back. In the cellar, *in toto*, your boy is home. He's only got to concentrate on that target, his mind is trained to take in that one object, just the target. But once he gets out on a wide ball field, and a crowd is yelling in his ears, and there's two or three men on bases jumpin' back and forth behind him his mind has got to do a lot of things at once, he's in a strange place, he gets panicky, he gets paralysed, he gets mad at the base runners and he's through! From that minute he can't pitch worth a nickel bag of cold peanuts!

He gets up, pulls down his vest. **David** *and* **Pat** *sit dumbly,* **Amos** *staring at nothing.*

Augie   I got to make a train, Mr Beeves.

Pat (*slowly rises. As though in a dream*)   I didn't want to waste the winters, that's why I trained him down the cellar.

Augie (*thoughtfully*)   Yeh, that's just where you made your mistake, Mr Beeves.

David (*rises*)   But. . . that was his plan. He didn't want to waste the winters. Down the cellar . . . it seemed like such a good idea!

Augie   But it was a mistake.

David   But he's been doing it twelve years! A man can't be multiplying the same mistake for twelve years, can he?

Augie   I guess he can, son. It was a very big mistake.

Pause.

Pat   Well . . . you can't take that out of him? Your coaches and . . . everything?

Augie   There's no coach in the world can take out a boy's brain and set it back twelve years. Your boy is crippled up here. (*Taps his temple.*) I'm convinced.

David   But if you coached him right, if you drilled him day after day . . .

Augie   It would take a long, long time, and I personally don't believe he'll ever get rid of it.

Pat   You can't . . . you can't try him, eh?

Augie   I know how you feel, Mr Beeves, but I am one man who will not take a boy out of his life when I know in my heart we're going to throw him away like a wet rag.

David (*for a long time he stands staring*)   He has no life.

Augie (*bends closer to hear*)   Eh?

David   He doesn't know how to do anything else.

Augie (*nods with sympathy*)   That was another mistake. (*He starts to turn away to go.*)

Pat (*as though to call him back somehow*)   I believed if he concentrated . . . concentration . . . You see I myself always jumped from one thing to another and never got anywhere, and I thought . . .

Augie   Yeh . . . when it works, concentration is a very sound principle. (*Takes a breath.*) Well, lots of luck.

Still unable to believe, **Pat** *can't speak.*

Augie   'Bye, Amos.

Amos *nods slightly, numbly staring.*

Augie (*at the door, to* **David**)   'Bye. (*He starts to open the door.*)

David   Look . . . (*He hurries to him. He looks in his eyes, his hand raised as though to grab the man and hold him here.*)

Augie   Yeh?

David *starts to speak, then looks at* **Amos** *who is still staring at nothing.* **David** *turns back to* **Augie**.

David . . . You'll see him in the leagues.

Augie I hope so. I just don't . . .

David (*trying to restrain his fury*) No, you'll see him. You're not the only team, you know. You'll see him in the leagues.

Augie (*grasps **David**'s arm*) . . . Take it easy, boy. (*To the others.*) I hope you'll pardon me for being late.

David (*quietly, like an echo, his voice cracking*) You'll see him.

Augie *nods. Glances at* **Pat** *and* **Amos**, *opens the door and goes.* **Pat** *and* **David** *stand looking at the door.* **Pat** *turns now, walks slowly to* **Amos**, *who is sitting. As* **Pat** *nears him he stands slowly, his fists clenched at his sides.*

Pat (*softly, really questioning*) He can be wrong too, can't he? (**Amos** *is silent, his face filling with hate.*) Can't he be wrong? (*No reply.*) He can, can't he?

Amos (*a whip-like shout*) No, he can't be!

Pat But everybody makes mistakes.

Amos (*with a cry he grabs* **Pat** *by the collar and shakes him violently back and forth*) Mistakes! Mistakes! You and your goddam mistakes!

David (*leaps to them, trying to break his grip*) Let him go! Amos, let him go!

Amos (*to* **Pat**, *amid his own and* **Pat**'s *weeping*) You liar! I'll kill you, you little liar, *you liar*!

With a new burst of violence he starts forcing **Pat** *backwards and down to the floor.* **Gus** *comes in as* **David** *locks an arm around* **Amos**'s *neck and jerks him from* **Pat** *who falls to the floor.*

Amos Leave me alone! Leave me alone!

With a great thrust **David** *throws* **Amos** *to the couch and stands over him, fists raised.* **Hester** *unnoticed enters and stands watching the scene.*

David Stay there! Don't get up! You'll fight me, Amos!

Pat (*scurrying to his feet, and taking* **David** *away from the couch*)
Don't, don't fight! (*He turns quickly, pleadingly to* **Amos**, *who is
beginning to sob on the couch.*) Amos, boy, boy . . . (**Amos** *lies across
the couch and sobs violently.* **Pat** *leans over and pats his head.*) Boy, boy.

Amos *swings his arm out blindly and hits* **Pat** *across the chest.* **David**
starts towards them but **Pat** *remains over him, patting his back.*

Pat   Come on, boy, please, boy, stop now, stop, Amos! Look,
Ame, look, I'll get Cleveland down here, I'll go myself, I'll
bring a man. Ame, listen, I did what I could, a man makes
mistakes, he can't figure on everything . . . (*He begins shaking*
Amos *who continues sobbing.*) Ame, stop it! (*He stands and begins
shouting over* **Amos**'s *sobbing.*) I admit it, I admit it, Ame, I lie,
I talk too much, I'm a fool, I admit it, but look how you pitch,
give me credit for that, give me credit for something! (*Rushes at*
Amos *and turns him over.*) Stop that crying! God Almighty, what
do you want me to do?! I'm a fool, what can I do?!

David (*wrenches* **Pat** *away from the couch. Stands over* **Amos**)
Listen, you! (*Leans over and pulls* **Amos** *by the collar to a sitting
position.* **Amos** *sits limply, sobbing.*) He made a mistake. That's
over with. You're going to drill on base play. You got a whole
life. One mistake can't ruin a life. He'll go to Cleveland. I'll
send him to New York . . .

Hester *enters quietly.*

David   The man can be wrong. Look at me! The man can
be wrong, you understand!

Amos *shakes his head.*

Amos   He's right.

David *releases him and stands looking down at him.* **Amos** *gets up
slowly, goes to a chair and sits.*

Amos   He's right. I always knew I couldn't play the bases.
Everything the man said was right. I'm dumb, that's why. I can't
figure nothin'. (*Looks up at* **Pat**.) There wasn't no time, he said,
no time for nothin' but throwin' that ball. Let 'em laugh, he
said, you don't need to know how to figure. He knew it all.

He knows everything! Well, this is one time I know something. I ain't gonna touch a baseball again as long as I live!

Pat (*frantically*)   Amos, you don't know what you're saying . . . !

Amos   I couldn't ever stand out on a diamond again! I can't do it! I know! I can't! (*Slight pause.*) I ain't goin' to let you kid me any more. I'm through. (*He rises.* **Pat** *sobs into his hands.*)

David (**Amos** *keeps shaking his head in denial of everything*)   What do you mean, through? Amos, you can't lay down. Listen to me. Stop shaking your head – who gets what he wants in this world?!

Amos (*suddenly*)   You. Only you.

David   Me! Don't believe it, Amos. (*Grabs him.*) Don't believe that any more!

Amos   Everything you ever wanted . . . in your whole life, every . . . !

David   Including my children, Ame? (*Silence.*) Where are my children!

Hester   Dave.

David (*to* **Hester**)   I want to tell him! (*To* **Amos**.) What good is everything when nothing is good without children? Do you know the laughing stock it makes of everything you do in the world? You'll never meet a man who doesn't carry one curse . . . at least one. Shory, JB, Pop, you, and me too. Me as much as anybody!

Hester   Don't, Davey . . .

David (*with a dreadful triumph*)   No, Hess, I'm not afraid of it any more. I want it out. I was always afraid I was something special in the world. But not after this. (*To* **Amos**.) *Nobody* escapes, Ame! But I don't lay down, I don't die because I'll have no kids. A man is born with one curse at least to be cracked over his head. I see it now, and you got to see it. Don't envy me, Ame. . . we're the same now. The world is made that way, as if a law was written in the sky somewhere – nobody escapes! (*Takes* **Amos**'s *hand.*)

Hester (*almost weeping she cannot restrain*)   Why do you talk that way?

David   Hess, the truth . . .

Hester   It's not the truth! . . . You have no curse! None at all!

David (*struck*)   What . . .

Hester   I wanted to wait till the scout signed him up. And then . . . when the house was full of noise and cheering, I'd stand with you on the stairs high over them all, and tell them you were going to have a child. (*With anger and disappointment and grief.*) Oh Davey, I saw you so proud . . .

David (*twisted and wracked, he bursts out*)   Oh, Hess, I am, I am.

Hester   No, you don't want it. I don't know what's happened to you, you don't want it now!

David (*with a chill of horror freezing him*)   Don't say that! Hester, you mustn't . . . (*He tries to draw her to him.*)

Hester (*holding him away*)   You've got to want it, Davey. You've just got to want it!

She bursts into tears and rushes out. He starts after her, calling her name . . . when he finds himself facing **Amos**.

Amos   Nobody escapes . . . (**David** *stops, turns to* **Amos**.) except you. (*He walks to the door, past* **David**, *and goes out.*)

Curtain.

Act Three

Scene One

Living room. Night in the following February.

JB *is asleep on the couch.* **Shory** *and* **Gus** *are silently playing cards and smoking at a table near the fireplace. Snow can be seen on the window muntins. Several coats on the rack. Presently . . .*

Gus   There's no brainwork in this game. Let me teach you claviash.

Shory   I can win all the money I need in rummy and pinochle. Play.

Gus   You have no intellectual curiosity.

Shory   No, but you can slip me a quarter. (*Showing his hand.*) Rummy.

Enter **Belle** *from the stairs.*

Gus (*to* **Belle**)   Everything all right?

Belle (*half turns to him, holding blanket forth*)   She keeps sweating up all the blankets. That poor girl.

Gus   The doctor says anything?

Belle   Yes . . . (*Thinks.*) He said, go down and get a dry blanket.

Gus   I mean, about when it will be coming along?

Belle   Oh, you can't tell about a baby. That's one thing about them, they come most any time. Sometimes when you don't expect it, and sometimes when you do expect it. (*She goes up to door and turns again.*) Why don't Davey buy a baby carriage?

Gus   Didn't he? I suppose he will.

Belle   But how can you have a baby without a baby carriage?

Shory   You better blow your nose.

Belle   I haven't time! (*She blows her nose and goes out, up left.*)

Shory   A quarter says it's a boy. (*Tosses a quarter on the table.*)

Gus   It's a bet. You know, statistics show more girls is born than boys. You should've asked me for odds.

Shory   Dave Beeves doesn't need statistics, he wants a boy. Matter of fact, let's raise it – a dollar to your half that he's got a boy tonight.

Gus   Statistically I would take the bet, but financially I stand pat.

Enter **David** *from left door to outside. He is dressed for winter. It is immediately evident that a deep enthusiasm, a ruddy satisfaction is upon him. He wears a strong smile. He stamps his feet a little as he removes his gloves, and then his short coat, muffler, hat, leaving a sweater on. As he closes the door . . .*

David   How'm I doing upstairs?

Gus   So far she only sweats.

David   Sweating! Is that normal?

Gus   Listen, she ain't up there eating ice cream.

David (*goes to the fireplace, rubs his hands before it. Of* **JB**, *as though amused*)   The least little thing happens and he stays home from work. He's been here all day.

Gus   Certain men like to make holidays. A new kid to him is always a holiday.

David (*he looks around*)   What a fuss.

Gus   You're very calm. Surprising to me. Don't you feel nervous?

Shory (*to* **Gus**)   You seen too many movies. What's the use of him pacing up and down?

David (*with an edge of guilt*)   I got the best doctor; everything she needs. I figure, whatever's going to happen'll happen. After all, I can't . . .

Breaks off. In a moment **Belle** *enters from the left door, carrying a different blanket. She goes towards the stair landing.* **David** *finally speaks, unable to restrain it.*

David   Belle . . . (*She stops. He goes to her, restraining anxiety.*) Would you ask the doctor . . . if he thinks it's going to be very hard for her, heh?

Belle   He told me to shut up.

David   Then ask JB's wife.

Belle   She told me to shut up too. But I'll ask her.

Belle *goes up the stairs.* **David** *watches her ascend a moment.*

David (*looking upstairs*)   That girl is going to live like a queen after this. (*Turns to them, banging his fist in his palm.*) Going to make a lot of money this year.

Shory   Never predict nothin' but the weather, half an hour ahead.

David   Not this time. I just finished mating my mink, and I think every one of them took.

Gus   All finished? That's fine.

A knock is heard on the door. **David** *goes to it, opens it.* **Pat** *enters. He is dressed in a pea jacket, a stocking-wool hat on his head. He carries a duffle bag on his shoulder.*

David   Oh, hello, Dad.

Pat   The baby come yet?

David   Not yet.

Pat   My train doesn't leave for a couple of hours. I thought I'd wait over here.

David   Here, give me that. (*He takes the duffle bag from* **Pat**, *puts it out of the way.*)

Shory   So you're really going, Pat?

Pat   I got my old job back – ship's cook. I figure with a little studying, maybe in a year or so, I'll have my Third licence. So . . .

David   It's so foolish your leaving, Dad. Can't I change your mind?

Pat   It's better this way, David. Maybe if I'm not around Amos'll take hold of himself.

There is a knock on the door.

David   That's probably Amos now.

He goes to the door, opens it. **Amos** *enters. He is smoking a cigarette.*

David   Hello, Ame. All locked up? Come in.

Amos   I got my motor running. Hello, Gus, Shory. (*He ignores* **Pat**. *There is a pause.*)

Gus   Working hard?

Amos (*a tired, embittered chuckle*)   Yeh, pretty tough; pumpin' gas, ringin' the cash register . . . (*Giving* **David** *a small envelope and a key.*) There's twenty-six bucks in there. I got the tally slip in with it.

David (*as though anxious for his participation; strained*)   Twenty-six! We did all right today.

Amos   Always do, don't ya? 'Night. (*Starts to go.*)

David   Listen, Ame. (**Amos** *turns.*) The mink'll be bearing in about a month. I was thinking you might like to take a shot at working with me, here . . . it's a great exercise . . . Spring is coming, you know. You want to be in condition . . .

Amos   For what?

David   Well . . . maybe play some ball this summer.

Amos (*glances at* **Pat**)   Who said I'm playing ball?

David (*as carelessly as possible*)   What are you going to do with yourself?

Amos   Pump your gas . . . Bring you the money every night.
Wait for something good to happen. (*A bitter little laugh.*) I mean,
the day they announced they're building the new main highway
right past your gas station I knew *something* good had to happen
to me. (*Laughing*) I mean it just *had* to, Dave! (*Now with real
feeling*) Baby hasn't come yet? (**David** *shakes his head, disturbed
by his brother's bitterness.*) Overdue, ain't she? (*Takes a drag on his
cigarette.*)

David   A little.

Amos   Well, if it's a boy . . . (*Glancing at* **Pat** *and defiantly
blowing out smoke.*) Don't have him pitchin' down the cellar.

With a wink at **David**, *he goes out. After a moment* **David** *goes to*
Pat.

David   Why must you go, Dad? Work with me here, I've
plenty for everybody, I don't need it all.

Pat   Inhaling cigarettes in those glorious lungs. I couldn't
bear to watch him destroying my work that way.

Shory (*at the fireplace*)   Come on, Pat, pinochle.

David (*beckoning* **Gus** *over to the right*)   Hey, Gus, I want to talk
to you.

Pat (*going to* **Shory**. *Without the old conviction*)   Fireplace heat is
ruination to the arteries.

Pat *takes* **Gus**'s *place,* **Gus** *coming to the right.*

Shory (*mixing the deck*)   So you'll drop dead warm. Sit down.
(*He deals.*)

David *and* **Gus** *are at right.* **JB** *continues sleeping. The card game
begins.*

David   I want you to do something for me, Gus. In a little
more than thirty days I'll have four or five mink for every bitch
in those cages. Four to one.

Gus   Well, don't count the chickens.

David   No, about this I'm sure. I want to mortgage the shop. Before you answer . . . I'm not being an Indian giver. I signed sixty per cent of the shop over to you because you're worth it – I didn't want what don't belong to me and I still don't. I just want you to sign so I can borrow some money on the shop. I need about twenty-five hundred dollars.

Gus   I can ask why?

David   Sure. I want to buy some more breeders.

Gus   Oh. Well, why not use the money you have?

David   Frankly, Gus . . . (*Laughs confidently.*) I don't have any other money.

Gus   Ah, go on now, don't start kidding me . . .

David   No, it's the truth. I've damn near as many mink out there as Dan Dibble. That costs big money. What do you say?

Pat *and* **Shory** *look up now and listen while playing their hand.*

Gus (*thinks a moment*)   Why do you pick on the shop to mortgage? You could get twenty-five hundred on the gas station, or the quarry, or the farm . . . (*Slight pause.*)

David   I did. I've got everything mortgaged. Everything but the shop.

Gus (*shocked*)   Dave, I can't believe this!

David (*indicates out of the right window*)   Well, look at them out there. I've got a *ranch*. You didn't think I had enough cash to buy that many, did you?

Gus (*gets up, trying to shake off his alarm*)   But, Dave, this is mink. Who knows what can happen to them? I don't understand how you can take everything you own and sink it in . . .

David   Four for one, Gus. If prices stay up I can make sixty thousand dollars this year.

Gus   But how can you be sure? You can't . . .

David   I'm sure.

Gus   But how can you be . . . ?

David (*more nervously now, wanting to end this tack*)   I'm sure. Isn't it possible? To be sure?

Gus   Yes, but why? (*Pause.*) Why are you sure?

JB (*suddenly erupting on the couch*)   Good God and . . . ! (*He sits up, rubbing himself*) What happened to those radiators you were going to put into this house? (*He gets up, goes to the fire, frozen.*) You could hang meat in this room.

David (*to* **JB**)   You're always hanging meat.

Gus   I don't know how to answer you. I have worked very hard in the shop . . . I . . . (*His reasonableness breaks.*) You stand there and don't seem to realise you'll be wiped out if those mink go, and now you want more yet!

David   *I said they're not going to die!*

JB (*to* **Pat** *and* **Shory**)   Who's going to die? What're they talking about?

David   Nothin'. (*He looks out of the window.* **JB** *Watches him, mystified.*)

Pat   I think Amos would smoke a pipe instead of those cigarettes, if you told him, Shory.

JB   Dave, you want a baby carriage, y'know.

David (*half turns*)   Heh? . . . Yey, sure.

JB   I figured you forgot to ask me so I ordered a baby carriage for you.

David *turns back to the window as* . . .

JB   Matter of fact, it's in the store. (*With great enthusiasm.*) Pearl grey! Nice soft rubber tyres too . . . Boy, one thing I love to see.

David (*turns to him, restraining*)   All right, will you stop talking?

JB *is shocked. In a moment he turns and goes to the rack, starts getting into his coat.* **David** *crosses quickly to him.*

David   Oh, John, what the hell! (*He takes* **JB***'s arm.*)

JB   You unnerve me, Dave! You unnerve me! A man acts a certain way when he's going to be a father, and by Jesus I want him to act that way.

Shory   Another moviegoer! Why should he worry about something he can't change?

David   I've got a million things to think of, John. I want to ask you.

JB   What?

David (*hangs* **JB***'s coat up*)   I want to get a buy on a new Buick; maybe you can help me swindle that dealer you know in Burley. I'm taking Hester to California in about a month. Sit down.

JB (*suddenly pointing at him*)   That's what unnerves me! You don't seem to realise what's happening. You can't take a month-old baby in a car to California.

David (*a blank, shocked look*)   Well, I meant . . .

JB (*laughs, slaps his back, relieved at this obvious truth*)   The trouble with you is, you don't realise that she didn't swell up because she swallowed an olive! (**Gus** *and he laugh;* **David** *tries to.*) You're a poppa, boy! You're the guy he's going to call Pop!

There is a commotion of footsteps upstairs. **David** *goes quickly to the landing.* **Belle** *hurries down. She is sniffling, sobbing.*

David   What happened?

Belle *touches his shoulder kindly but brushes right past him to the fireplace where she picks up a wood basket.*

David (*continues going to her*)   What happened, Belle!

Belle (*standing with the wood*)   She's having it, she's having it. (*She hurries to the landing,* **David** *behind her.*)

David   What does the doctor say? Belle! How is she? (*He catches her arm.*)

Belle   I don't know. She shouldn't have fallen that time. She shouldn't have fallen, Davey. Oh dear.

She bursts into a sob and rushes upstairs. **David** *stands gaping upwards. But* **Gus** *is staring at* **David.** *After a long moment . . .*

Gus (*quietly*)   Hester fell down?

David (*turns slowly to him after an instant of his own*)   What?

Gus   Hester had a fall?

David   Yeh, some time ago.

Gus   You had her to the doctor?

David   Yeh.

Gus   He told you the baby would be possibly dead? (*Pause.*)

David   What're you talking about?

Gus (*quavering*)   I think you know what I'm talking about.

David *is speechless. Walks to a chair and sits on the arm as though, at the price of terrible awkwardness, to simulate ease. Always glancing at* **Gus,** *he gets up unaccountably, and in a broken, uncontrolled voice . . .*

David   What are you talking about?

Gus   I understand why you were so sure about the mink. But I sign no mortgage on the shop. I do not bet on dead children.

David *is horrified at the revelation. He stands rigidly, his fists clenched. He might sit down or spring at* **Gus** *or weep.*

JB   He couldn't think a thing like that. He . . .

He looks to **David** *for reinforcement, but* **David** *is standing there hurt and silent and self-horrified.* **JB** *goes to* **David.**

JB   Dave, you wouldn't want a thing like that. (*He shakes him.*) Dave!

David (*glaring at* **Gus**)   I'd cut my throat!

He walks downstage from **JB,** *looking at* **Gus.** *His movements are wayward, restless, like one caught in a strange cul-de-sac.* **Gus** *is silent.*

David   Why do you look at me that way? (*Glances at* **JB**, *then slowly back to* **Gus**.) Why do you look that way? I'm only telling you what happened. A person has to look at facts, doesn't he? I heard something at the door and I opened it . . . and there she was lying on the step. A fact is a fact, isn't it? (*They don't reply. Bursting out.*) Well, for Jesus' sake, if you . . . !

Gus (*a shout*)   What fact! She fell! So the baby is dead because she fell? Is this a fact?!

David (*moves away from* **Gus**'s *direction, in high tension*)   I didn't say dead. It doesn't have to be dead to be . . . to . . . (*Breaks off.*)

Gus   To be what?

Pause.

David   To be a curse on us. It can come wrong . . . A fall can make them that way. The doctor told me. (**Gus** *looks unconvinced.*) The trouble with you is that you think I got a special angel watching over me.

Shory (*pointing at* **Gus**)   He said it that time, brother!

Gus (*to* **Shory** *too*)   A man needs a special angel to have a live child?

David (*furiously*)   Who said he was going to be dead?!

Gus   What are you excited about? (*Takes his arm.*) Take it easy, sit . . .

David (*freeing his arm*)   Stop humouring me, will you? Dan Dibble'll have my new mink here tonight. I got all the papers ready . . . (*Goes to a drawer, takes out papers.*) All you do is sign and . . .

Gus (*suddenly he rushes to* **David**, *pulls the papers out of his hand, throws them down*)   Are you mad?! (*He frightens* **David** *into immobility.*) There is no catastrophe upstairs, there is no guarantee up there for your mink. (*He grasps* **David**'s *arm, pleadingly.*) Dave . . .

David   If you say that again I'm going to throw you out of this house!

JB (*nervously*)   Oh, come on now, come on now.

From above a scream of pain is heard. **David** *freezes.* **Gus** *looks up.*

Gus (*to* **David**)   Don't say that again.

David *thrusts his hands into his pockets as though they might reveal him too. Under great tension he attempts to speak reasonably. His voice leaps occasionally, he clears his throat.* **Gus** *never takes his eyes off him.* **David** *walks from* **JB**, *unwillingly.*

David   I'm a lucky man, John. Everything I've ever gotten came . . . straight out of the blue. There's nothing mad about it. It's facts. When I couldn't have Hester unless old man Falk got out of the way, he was killed just like it was specially for me. When I couldn't fix the Marmon a man walks in from the middle of the night . . . and fixes it for me. I buy a lousy little gas station . . . they build a highway in front of it. That's lucky. You pay for that.

Shory   Damn right you do.

Gus   Where is such a law?

David   I don't know. (*Observes a silence. He walks to the windows.*) Of all the people I've heard of I'm the only one who's never paid. Well . . . I think the holiday's over. (*Turns towards upstairs, with great sorrow.*) I think we're about due to join up with the rest of you. I'll have almost sixty thousand dollars when I market my mink . . . but it won't be money I got without paying for it. And that's why I put everything in them. That's why I'm sure. Because from here on in we're paid for. I saw it in black and white when she fell. (*With a heartbroken tone.*) God help me, we're paid for now. I'm not afraid of my luck any more, and I'm going to play it for everything it's worth.

Gus   David, you break my heart. This is from Europe, this idea. This is from Asia, from the rotten places, not America.

David   No?

Gus   Here you are not a worm, a louse in the earth; here you are a man. A man deserves everything here!

Shory   Since when?

Gus (*strongly, to* **Shory**)   Since forever!

Shory   Then I must have been born before that.

Gus (*angrily now*)   I beg your pardon he is not you and do me a favour and stop trying to make him like you.

David   He's not making me anything.

Gus   He won't be happy until he does, I can tell you! (*Indicating* **Shory**.) This kind of people never are.

Shory   What kind of people?

Gus   Your kind! His life he can make golden, if he wants.

Shory   Unless the walls blow out.

Gus   If he don't go chasing after whores his walls won't blow out. (*Quietly.*) And I beg your pardon. I didn't mean nothing personal.

JB (*goes to* **David**)   I'll lend you the money for the mink, Dave.

Gus   Are you mad?

JB   I can see what he means, Gus. (*Looks at* **David**.) It takes a great kind of man to prepare himself that way. A man does have to pay. It's just the way it happens, senseless. (*He glances upstairs, then to* **David**.) It's true. It always happens senseless. I'll back you, Dave.

David   I'd like to pay him tonight if I can.

They all turn to look up as **Belle** *appears, slowly descending the stairs. They do not hear her until she is a little way down. Her usual expression of wide-eyed bewilderment is on her face, but now she is tense, and descends looking at* **David**. *She half sniffs, half sobs into her kerchief. She stops on the stairs.* **David** *rises. She half laughs, half snivels in a quiet ecstasy of excitement, and weakly motions him upstairs. He comes towards her questioningly, to the landing.*

Belle   Go . . . Go up.

David   What? What . . . ?

Belle (*suddenly bursts out and rushes down and flings her arms about him*)   Oh, Davey, Davey.

David (*ripping her free, he roars in her face*)   What happened?! (*With a sob of grief in his voice, he grips her.*) Belle!

The cry of a baby is suddenly heard from above. The sound almost throws **David** *back, away from the stairs. He stands stock still, hard as a rock, looking upward, his mouth fallen open.*

Belle (*still half sobbing*)   It's a boy. A perfect baby boy!

She now breaks into full sobs and rushes up the stairs. Everything is still a moment, **David** *stares at nothing. The cry sounds again. He looks upward again as though to let it sink in.* **JB** *goes to him, hand extended.*

JB (*filled with joy, and gravely*)   Dave.

David *dumbly shakes his hand, a weak smile on his face.*

Gus   It's the first time you've been right since I knew you.

JB   A boy, a boy, Dave! Just what you wanted!

A strange short laugh leaps from **David**. *An easier but still tense laugh comes.* **Pat** *goes to him and shakes his hand.*

Pat   Dave, a new generation!

Gus (*smilingly*)   Well? You see? (*Laughs.*) A good man gets what a good man makes. (*Hits* **David** *jovially.*) Wake up now! Good luck! (*He tosses a quarter to* **Shory**.) It's the first time you've been right since I knew you.

JB   Come out of the ether. Take a look at her, Dave.

David *rushes out. They stand astonished for a moment.*

JB   What do you suppose come over him?

Gus   What else could come over him?. . . He's ashamed.

Gus *hurries out the door. The others remain in silence. Then one by one they look upstairs towards the sound of the baby's crying.*

Slow curtain.

Scene Two

Before the curtain rises thunder is heard.

It is one month later. The living room. Night.

The room is empty and in darkness. A bolt of lightning illuminates it through the windows, then darkness again. Now the door to the outside opens and **Hester** *enters. She is very tense but her motions are minute, as though she were mentally absorbed and had entirely forgotten her surroundings. Without removing her coat or galoshes she comes to the centre of the room and stands there staring. Then she goes to a window and looks out. A flash of lightning makes her back a step from the window; and without further hesitation she goes to the phone, switching on a nearby light.*

Hester (*she watches the window as she waits*)   Hello? Gus? Where have you been, I've been ringing you for an hour. (*She listens.*) Well, look, could you come over here? Right now, I mean. It would *not* be interfering, Gus, I want to talk to you. He's outside. Gus, you've got to come here – his mink are going to die. (*She keeps glancing at the window.*) He doesn't know it yet, but he'll probably see it any minute. Dan Dibble called before . . . He's lost over thirty of his already . . . They use the same fish. I want you here when he notices. (*She turns suddenly towards the door.*) He's coming in. You hurry over now . . . Please!

She hangs up, and starts for the door, but as though to compose herself she stops, and starts towards a chair when she realises she still has her coat and galoshes on. She is kicking off the galoshes when **David** *enters. He looks up at her, and with a slight glance upstairs . . .*

David   Everything all right?

Hester   Why?

David   I thought I heard a call or a scream.

Hester   No, there was no scream.

David   I guess it was the lightning. Is he all right? (*Of the baby.*)

Hester   There's no gate there, you can go up and see.

David   How can I go to him with my hands so bloody? (*She turns from him. He starts for the door.*)

Hester   I thought you were through feeding.

David   I am. I'm just grinding some for tomorrow.

Hester   Are they all right?

David   I never saw them so strung up. I think it's the hail banging on the cages. (*There is a momentary hiatus as he silently asks for leave to go.*) I just wondered if he was all right. (*He takes a step.*)

Hester (*suddenly*)   Don't go out again, Davey. Please. You told me yourself, they ought to be left alone when they're whelping.

David   I've got to be there, Hess, I've just got to. I . . . (*He goes to her.*) I promise you, after they whelp we'll go away, we'll travel . . . I'm going to make a queen's life for you.

Hester   Don't go out.

David   I'll be in right away . . .

Hester (*grasps his arms*)   I don't want them to be so important, Davey!

David   But everything we've got is in them. You know that.

Hester   I'm not afraid of being poor . . .

David   That's 'cause you never were – and you'll never be. You're going to have a life like a . . .

Hester   Why do you keep saying that? I don't want it, I don't need it! I don't care what happens out there! And I don't want you to care. Do you hear what I say, I don't want you to care!

A bolt of lightning floods suddenly through the windows. **David** *starts. Then hurries to the door.*

Hester (*frightened now*)   Davey! (**David** *stops, does not turn.*) You can't stop the lightning, can you? (*He does not turn still. She goes closer to him, pleading.*) I know how hard you worked, but it won't be the first year's work that ever went for nothing in the world. It happens that way, doesn't it?

David (*he turns to her slowly. Now his emotions seem to flood him*)
Not when a man doesn't make any mistakes. I kept them alive
all year. Not even one got sick. I didn't make a mistake. And
now this storm comes, just when I need it calm, just tonight . . .

Hester   You talk as though the sun were shining everywhere
else but here, as though the sky is making thunder just to knock
you down.

David (*he looks at her long as though she had reached into him*)   Yeh,
that's the way I talk. (*He seems about to sob.*) Bear with me, Hess –
only a little while. (*He moves to go.*)

Hester   Davey . . . the house is grey. Like the old paint was
creeping back on the walls. When will we sit and talk again?
When will you pick up the baby . . . ?

David (*comes alive*)   I did, Hess.

Hester   You never did. And why is that?

David   When you were out of the house.

Hester   Never, not since he's been born. Can't you tell me
why? (**David** *turns and opens the door. Her fear raises her voice.*) Can't
you tell me why? (*He starts out.*) Davey, tell me why! (*He goes out.
She calls out the door.*) Davey, I don't understand! Come back
here!

*In a moment, she comes away, closing the door. Her hands are lightly
clasped to her throat. She comes to a halt in the room; now she turns on
another lamp. She suddenly hears something behind her, turns and takes
a step towards the door as* **Gus** *quietly enters.*

Hester (*relieved*)   Oh, Gus!

Gus (*glancing towards the door*)   Is he coming right back?

Hester   He goes in and out, I don't know. You'll stay here
tonight, won't you?

Gus   The first thing to do is sit down.

As he leads her to the couch – she is near tears.

Hester   I kept calling you and calling you.

Gus (*taking off his coat*)   Now get hold of yourself; there's nothing to do till he finds out. I'm sorry, I was in Burley all afternoon, I just got home. What did Dibble tell you? (*He returns to her.*)

Hester   Just that he was losing animals, and he thought it was silkworm in the feed. They share the same carload.

Gus   Ah. David notices nothing? (*A gesture towards outside with his head.*)

Hester   He just says they're strung up, but that's the lightning. It takes time for them to digest.

Gus   Well then, we'll wait and see. (*He goes to the window, looks out.*) This storm is going to wipe out the bridges. It's terrible.

Hester   What am I going to do, Gus? He worked all year on those animals.

Gus   We will do what we have to, Hester, that's what we will do. (*He turns to her, taking out an envelope.*) Actually, I was coming over tonight anyway . . . To say goodbye.

Hester   Goodbye!

Gus   In here I explain. (*He places the envelope on the mantel.*) When I am gone, give it to him. I can't argue with him no more.

Hester   You mean you're moving away?

Gus   I am going to Chicago. There is an excellent position for me. Double what I can make here.

Hester   But why are you going?

Gus   I told you, I can make double . . .

Hester (*gets up*)   Don't treat me like a baby, why are you going? (*Slight pause.*)

Gus   Well . . . Actually, I am lonely. (*Laughs slightly.*) There is plenty of girls here, but no wifes, Hester. Thirty-seven years is a long time for a man to wash his own underwear.

Hester (*touched*)   You and your red-headed girls!

Gus   I was always a romantic man. You know that, don't you? Truly.

Hester   But to give up a business and go traipsing off just for . . . ?

Gus   Why not? What made me give up Detroit to come here?

Hester   Really, Gus?

Gus   Certainly. Moving is very necessary for me. (*Pause.*) I'm leaving tomorrow night.

Hester   But why? I suppose I should understand, but I can't. (*Pause.* **Gus** *looks directly at her.*) It doesn't make sense. (*Insistently.*) Gus?

Gus (*pause. For a long time he keeps her in his eye*)   Because I have no courage to stay here. (*Pause.*) I was talking today with a doctor in Burley. I believe David . . . is possibly losing his mind.

She does not react. She stands there gaping at him. He waits. With no sound she backs a few steps, then comes downstage and lightly sets both hands on the couch, never taking her eyes from him. A pause. As though hearing what he said again, she is impelled to move again, to a chair on whose back she sets a hand – facing him now. They stand so a moment.

I thought surely you knew. Or at least you would know soon. (*She does not answer.*) Do you know?

Hester   I've almost thought so sometimes . . . But I can't believe he . . .

Gus (*a new directness, now that she has taken the blow*)   I have been trying to straighten him out all month. But I have no more wisdom, Hester. I . . . I would like to take him to the doctors in Burley.

Hester (*shocked*)   Burley!

Gus   Tonight. They will know what to say to him there.

Hester (*horrified*)   No, he's not going there.

Gus   It is no disgrace. You are talking like a silly woman.

Hester   He's not going there! There's nothing wrong with him. He's worried, that's all.

Gus   When those animals begin dying he will be more than worried. Nothing worse could possibly happen . . .

Hester   No. If he can take the shock tonight he'll be all right. I think it's better if they die.

Gus   For God's sake, no!

Hester   All his life he's been waiting for it. All his life, waiting, waiting for something to happen. It'll be over now, all over, don't you see? Just stay here tonight. And when it happens, you'll talk to him.

Gus   What he has lost I can't put back, Hester. He is not a piece of machinery.

Hester (*stops moving*)   What has he lost? What do you mean, lost?

Gus   What a man must have, what a man must believe. That on this earth he is the boss of his life. Not the leafs in the teacups, not the stars. In Europe I seen already millions of Davids walking around, millions. They gave up already to know that they are the boss. They gave up to know that they deserve this world. And now here too, with such good land, with such a . . . such a big sky, they are saying . . . I hear it every day . . . that it is somehow unnatural for a man to have a sweet life and nice things. Daily they wait for catastrophe. A man must understand the presence of God in his hands. And when he don't understand it he is trapped. David is trapped, Hester. You understand why everything he has is in the mink?

Hester (*wide-eyed*)   It's the baby, isn't it? He thought it was going to be . . .

Gus   Dead, yes. Say, say out now. I was here that night. He always wanted so much to have a son and that is why he saw him dead. This, what he wanted most of all, he couldn't have.

This finally would be his catastrophe. And then everything would be guaranteed for him. And that is why he put everything in those animals.

Hester   Gus . . .

Gus   The healthy baby stole from David his catastrophe, Hester. Perfect he was born and David was left with every penny he owns in an animal that can die like this – (*snaps his fingers*) and the catastrophe still on its way.

Hester (*seeing the reason*)   He never touched the baby.

Gus   How can he touch him? He is bleeding with shame, Hester. Because he betrayed his son, and he betrayed you. And now if those animals die he will look into the tea leafs of his mind, into the sky he will look where he always looked, and if he sees retribution there . . . you will not call him worried any more. Let me take him to Burley before he notices anything wrong in the cages.

Hester   No. He's Davey, he's not some . . .

Gus   They will know what to do there!

Hester   I know what to do! (*She moves away and faces him.*) I could have warned him . . . Dan called before he started feeding.

Gus (*shocked and furious*)   Hester!

Hester   I wanted them dead! I want them dead now, those beautiful rats!

Gus   How could you do that!

Hester   He's got to lose. Once and for all he's got to lose. I always knew it had to happen, let it happen now, before the baby can see and understand. You're not taking him anywhere. He'll be happy again. It'll be over and he'll be happy!

Gus (*unwillingly*)   Hester.

Hester   No, I'm not afraid now. It'll be over now.

Gus   What will be over, Hester? He took out last week an insurance policy. A big one. (**Hester** *stops moving*) It covers his life.

Hester   No, Gus.

Gus   What will be over?

Hester (*a cry*)   No, Gus! (*Breaks into sobbing.*)

Gus (*taking her by the arms*)   Get hold now, get hold!

Hester (*sobbing, shaking her head negatively*)   Davey, Davey . . . he was always so fine, what happened to him . . . !

Gus   He mustn't see you this way . . . ! Nothing is worse than . . .

Hester (*trying to break from* **Gus** *to go out*)   Davey, Davey .

Gus   Stop it, Hester! He's shamed enough!

He has her face in his hands as the door suddenly opens and **David** *is standing there.* **Gus** *releases her. They stand apart.* **David** *has stopped moving in surprise. He looks at her, then at* **Gus**, *then at her.* **David** *goes towards her.*

David (*astonished, alarmed*)   Hess. What's the matter?

Hester   Nothing . . . How is everything outside?

David   It's still hailing . . . (*Stops. With an edge of self-accusation.*) Why were you crying?

Hester (*her voice still wet*)   I wasn't really.

David (*feeling the awkwardness, glances at both; to Gus*)   Why were you holding her?

Hester (*with an attempt at a laugh*)   He wasn't holding me. He's decided to go to Chicago and . . .

David (*mystified, to* **Gus**)   Chicago! Why . . .

Hester (*tries to laugh*)   He wants to find a wife! Imagine?

David (*to Gus*)   All of a sudden you . . . ?

Hester (*unbuttoning his coat, ready to weep and trying to be gay*)   Let's have some tea and sit up till way late and talk! Don't go out any more, Davey . . . From now on I'm not letting you out of my sight . . . There are so many nice things to talk about!

She has his coat and has just stepped away with a gross animation.

David (*deeply worried. Brushing her attempt away*)   Why were you crying, Hester?

The phone rings. **Hester** *fairly leaps at the sound. She starts quickly for the phone but* **David** *is close to it and picks it up easily, slightly puzzled at her frantic eagerness to take it.*

Hester   It's probably Ellie. I promised to lend her a hat for tomorrow.

David (*looks at her perplexed. He lifts the receiver.*)   Yes?

As he speaks **Hester** *steps away from him, in fear now.* **Gus** *changes position instinctively, almost as though for physical advantage.*

David   Mr Dibble? No, he isn't here; I don't expect him. Oh! Well, he isn't here yet. What's it all about? (*Listens.*) What are you talking about? Have I got what under control? (*Listens. Now with horror.*) Of course I've fed! Why didn't you call me, you know I feed before this! God damn your soul, you know I use the same feed he does! (*Roars.*) Don't tell me he called me! Don't . . . ! (*Listens*) When did he call?

Breaks off, listens. He turns, listening, to **Hester**; *slowly, an expression of horrified perplexity and astonishment grips his face. His eyes stay on* **Hester**.

David   Well, they seem all right now . . . maybe it hasn't had time to grip them. (*Still into the phone.*) Yeh . . . yeh, all right, I'll wait for him.

He hangs up weakly. For a long time he looks at her. Then he looks at **Gus** *and back to her as though connecting them somehow.*

David   What . . . Why . . . didn't you tell me he called?

Hester (*suddenly she dares not be too near him; she holds out a hand to touch and ward him off . . . she is a distance from him*)   Davey . . .

David   Why didn't you stop me from feeding?

Gus   Dan'll be here. Maybe he can do something.

David (*facing* **Hester**)   What can he do? Something's wrong in the feed! He can't pull it out of their stomachs! (*With welling grief. To* **Hester**.) Why didn't you tell me? (**Hester** *retreats a few inches.*) Why are you moving away from me? (*He suddenly reaches out and catches her arm.*) You wanted them to die!

Hester (*straining at his grip*)   You always said something had to happen. It's better this way, isn't it?

David   Better?! My boy is a pauper, we're on the bottom of a hole, how is it better!

Hester (*her fear alone makes her brave*)   Then I . . . I think I'll have to go away, Davey. I can't stay here, then.

She moves towards the stairs. He lets her move a few steps, then moves across to her and she stops and faces him.

David   You can't . . . What did you say?

Hester   I can't live with you, Davey. Not with the baby.

David   No, Hester.

Hester   I don't want him to see you this way. It's a harmful thing. I'm going away.

David (*he breathes as though about to burst into weeping. He looks to* **Gus**, *stares at him, then back to her. Incredibly*)   You're going with him?

Hester (*she darts a suddenly frightened glance towards* **Gus**)   Oh, no, no, I didn't mean that. He was going anyway.

David (*it is truer to him now*)   You're going with him.

Hester   No, David, I'm not going with anybody . . .

David (*with certainty. Anger suddenly stalks him*)   You're going with him!

Hester   No, Davey . . . !

David (*to* **Gus**)   You told her not to tell me!

Hester   He wasn't even here when Dan phoned!

David   How do I know where he was! (*To* **Gus**.) You think I'm a blind boy?!

Hester   You're talking like a fool!

David   You couldn't have done this to me! He wants you!

He starts to stride for **Gus**. **Hester** *gets in front of him.*

Hester   I did it! (*Grabs his coat.*) Davey, I did it myself!

David   No, you couldn't have! Not you! (*To* **Gus**.) You think I've fallen apart? You want her . . . ?

He starts to push her aside, knocking a chair over, going for **Gus**. *She slaps him hard across the face. He stops moving.*

Hester (*with loathing and heartbreak*)   I did it!

For an instant they are still, she watching for his reaction. He quietly draws in a sob, looking at her in grief.

I wanted you like you were, Davey – a good man, able to do anything. You were always a good man, why can't you understand that?

David   A good man! You pick up a phone and everything you've got dies in the ground! A man! What good is a man!

Hester   You can start again, start fresh and clean!

David   For what? For what?! The world is a madhouse, what can you build in a madhouse that won't be knocked down when you turn your back!

Hester   It was you made it all and you destroyed it! I'm going, Davey . . . (*With a sob.*) I can't bear any more. (*She rushes to the landing.*)

David (*a call, and yet strangled by sobs*)   Hester.

Hester *halts, looks at him. His hands raised towards her, shaken and weeping, he moves towards the landing frantically.*

David   I love you . . . I love you . . . Don't . . . don't . . . don't.

He reaches her, and sobbing, lost, starts drawing her down to him as the door, left, swings open. **Dan Dibble** *rushes in and halts when he sees* **David**. *He carries a small satchel.*

Dibble (*indicating downstage, right*)   I've been out there looking for you, what are you doing in here? I've got something may help them. Come on. (*He starts for the door.*)

David   I don't want to look at them, Dan. (*He goes to a chair.*)

Dibble   You can't be sure, it might take . . . (*Opens the door.*)

David   No, I'm sure they digested, it's over two hours.

Dibble (*stops moving suddenly at door*)   Over two hours what?

David   Since I fed them.

Dibble   You didn't give them this morning's load of fish?

David   What else could I give them? The load I split with you, goddamit.

Dibble   Well, you just couldn't've, David. They don't show a sign yet: that kind of silkworm'll kill them in twenty minutes. You must've . . .

David   Silkworm. – But my fish wasn't wormy . . .

Dibble   They don't look like worms, they're very small, you wouldn't have noticed them, they're black, about the size of a . . .

David   Poppyseed.

Dibble   A grain of ground pepper, yah. Come on . . . (*But* **David** *is motionless, staring . . .*) Well? You want me to look at them?

David *slowly sits in a chair.*

Gus   At least have a look, Dave. (*Slight pause.*)

David (*wondrously; but also an edge of apology*)   . . . I saw them, Dan. I didn't know what they were but I decided not to take any chances, so I threw them away.

Dibble (*angering*)   But you couldn't have gone over every piece of fish!

David   Well I . . . yah, I did, Dan. Most of it was okay, but the ones with the black specks I threw away.

Hester   Davey! – You saved them!

David   Well, you told me to watch the feed very carefully, Dan – I figured you'd notice them the same as me!

Dibble   But you know nobody's got the time to go over every goddam piece of fish!

David   But I thought everybody did! – I swear, Dan!

Dibble   God Almighty, Dave, a man'd think you'd warn him if you saw silkworm! – The least you could've done is call me.

David   I started to, I had the phone in my hand – but it seemed ridiculous, me telling you something. Listen, let me give you some of my breeders to start you off again.

Dibble   No – no . . .

David   Please, Dan, go out and pick whatever you like.

Dibble   . . . Well, I might think about that, but I'm too old to start all over again, I don't think I could get up the steam. Well, goodnight.

Dibble *exits.*

Gus *and* **Hester** *stand watching* **David***, who is puzzled and astonished.*

David   I can't believe it. He's the best in the business.

Gus   Not any more.

Hester   This wasn't something from the sky, dear. This was you only. You must see that now, don't you?

The baby crying is heard from above.

I'd better go up, he's hungry. Come up? – Why don't you, Dave?

David (*awkwardly*)   I will . . . right away. (**Hester** *exits. His face is rapt.*) But they couldn't all have made their own luck! – JB with his drinking, Shory with his whores, Dad and Amos . . . and you losing your shop. (*Seizing on it.*) And I could never have fixed that Marmon if you hadn't walked in like some kind of an angel! – That Marmon wasn't me!

Gus   You'd have towed it to Newton and fixed it there without me. (*Grasps* **David***'s hand.*) But is that really the question anyway? Of course bad things must happen. And you can't help it when God drops the other shoe. But whether you lay there or get up again – that's the part that's entirely up to you, that's for sure.

David   You don't understand it either, do you?

Gus   No, but I live with it. All I know is you are a good man, but also you have luck. So you have to grin and bear it – you are lucky!

David   For now.

Gus   Well, listen – 'for now' is a very big piece of 'forever'.

Hester (*from above*)   Dave? You coming up?

Gus   Go on, kiss the little fellow.

David   . . . I had the phone in my hand to call him. And I put it down. I had his whole ranch right here in my hand.

Gus   You mean you were a little bit like God . . . for him.

David   Yes. Except I didn't know it.

Gus (*a thumb pointing heavenward*)   Maybe He doesn't know either.

Hester (*from above*)   David? Are you there?

Gus   Goodnight, Dave.

David (*with a farewell wave to* **Gus**, *calls upstairs*)   Yes, I'm here!

He goes to the stairs. A shock of thunder strikes. He quickly turns towards the windows, the old apprehension in his face.

(*To himself.*) For now. (*With a self-energised determination in his voice and body.*) Comin' up!

As he mounts the stairs a rumble of thunder sounds in the distance.

Methuen Drama Student Editions

Methuen Drama Modern Plays

include work by

Edward Albee
Jean Anouilh
John Arden
Margaretta D'Arcy
Peter Barnes
Sebastian Barry
Brendan Behan
Dermot Bolger
Edward Bond
Bertolt Brecht
Howard Brenton
Anthony Burgess
Simon Burke
Jim Cartwright
Caryl Churchill
Noël Coward
Lucinda Coxon
Sarah Daniels
Nick Darke
Nick Dear
Shelagh Delaney
David Edgar
David Eldridge
Dario Fo
Michael Frayn
John Godber
Paul Godfrey
David Greig
John Guare
Peter Handke
David Harrower
Jonathan Harvey
Iain Heggie
Declan Hughes
Terry Johnson
Sarah Kane
Charlotte Keatley
Barrie Keeffe
Howard Korder

Robert Lepage
Doug Lucie
Martin McDonagh
John McGrath
Terrence McNally
David Mamet
Patrick Marber
Arthur Miller
Mtwa, Ngema & Simon
Tom Murphy
Phyllis Nagy
Peter Nichols
Sean O'Brien
Joseph O'Connor
Joe Orton
Louise Page
Joe Penhall
Luigi Pirandello
Stephen Poliakoff
Franca Rame
Mark Ravenhill
Philip Ridley
Reginald Rose
Willy Russell
Jean-Paul Sartre
Sam Shepard
Wole Soyinka
Simon Stephens
Shelagh Stephenson
Peter Straughan
C. P. Taylor
Theatre de Complicite
Theatre Workshop
Sue Townsend
Judy Upton
Timberlake Wertenbaker
Roy Williams
Snoo Wilson
Victoria Wood

Methuen Drama Contemporary Dramatists
include

John Arden (two volumes)
Arden & D'Arcy
Peter Barnes (three volumes)
Sebastian Barry
Dermot Bolger
Edward Bond (eight volumes)
Howard Brenton
  (two volumes)
Richard Cameron
Jim Cartwright
Caryl Churchill
  (two volumes)
Sarah Daniels (two volumes)
Nick Darke
David Edgar (three volumes)
David Eldridge
Ben Elton
Dario Fo (two volumes)
Michael Frayn (three volumes)
John Godber (three volumes)
Paul Godfrey
David Greig
John Guare
Lee Hall (two volumes)
Peter Handke
Jonathan Harvey
  (two volumes)
Declan Hughes
Terry Johnson (three volumes)
Sarah Kane
Barrie Keeffe
Bernard-Marie Koltès
  (two volumes)
David Lan
Bryony Lavery
Deborah Levy
Doug Lucie

David Mamet (four volumes)
Martin McDonagh
Duncan McLean
Anthony Minghella
  (two volumes)
Tom Murphy (five volumes)
Phyllis Nagy
Anthony Neilson
Philip Osment
Gary Owen
Louise Page
Stewart Parker (two volumes)
Joe Penhall
Stephen Poliakoff
  (three volumes)
David Rabe
Mark Ravenhill
Christina Reid
Philip Ridley
Willy Russell
Eric-Emmanuel Schmitt
Ntozake Shange
Sam Shepard (two volumes)
Wole Soyinka (two volumes)
Simon Stephens
Shelagh Stephenson
David Storey (three volumes)
Sue Townsend
Judy Upton
Michel Vinaver
  (two volumes)
Arnold Wesker (two volumes)
Michael Wilcox
Roy Williams (two volumes)
Snoo Wilson (two volumes)
David Wood (two volumes)
Victoria Wood